This Mandala Coloring book Belongs To

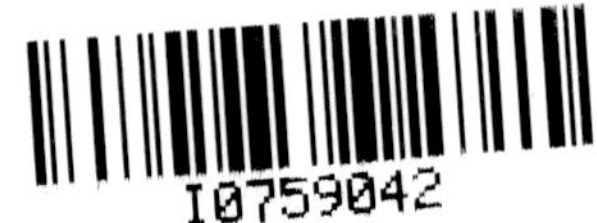

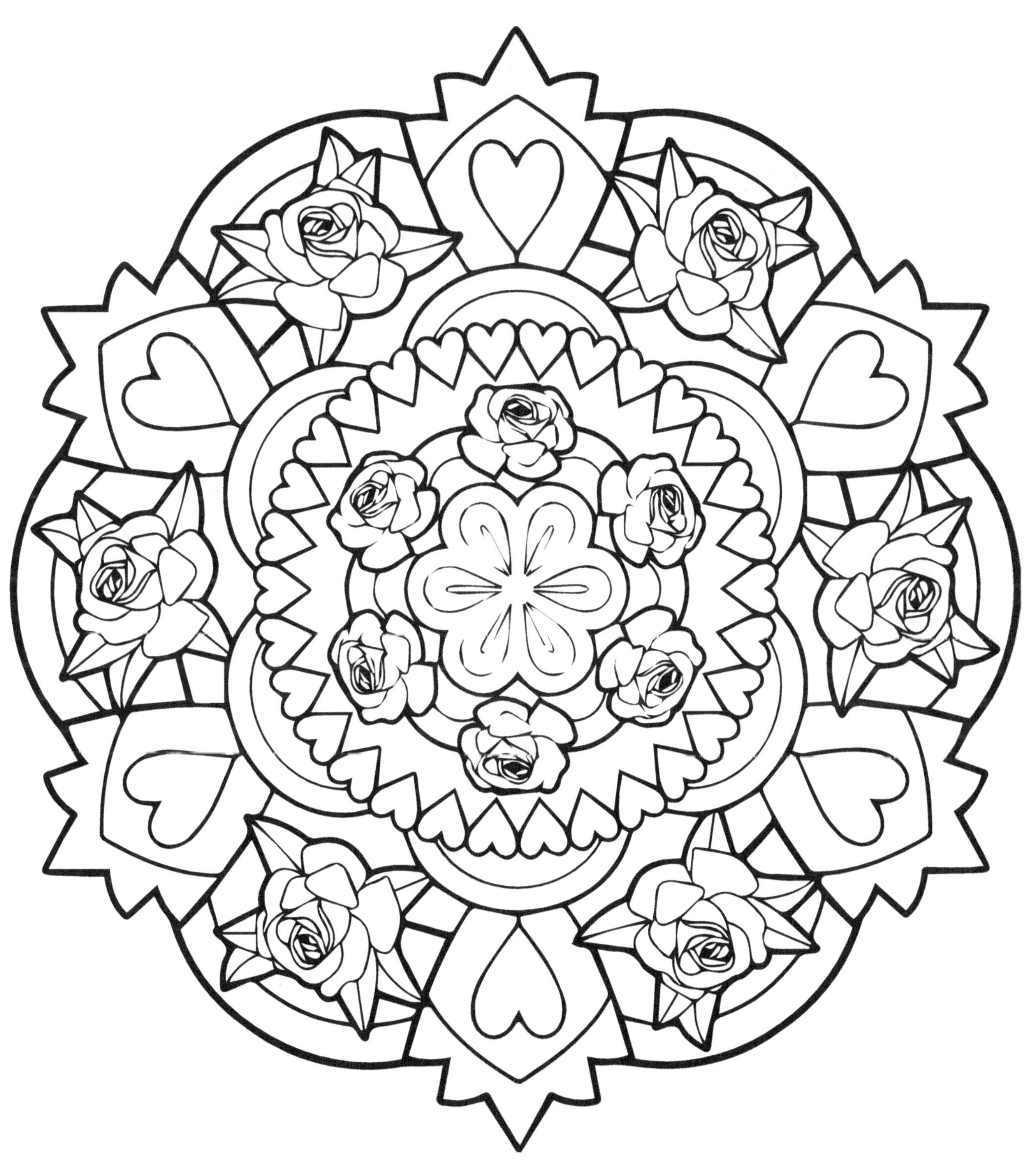

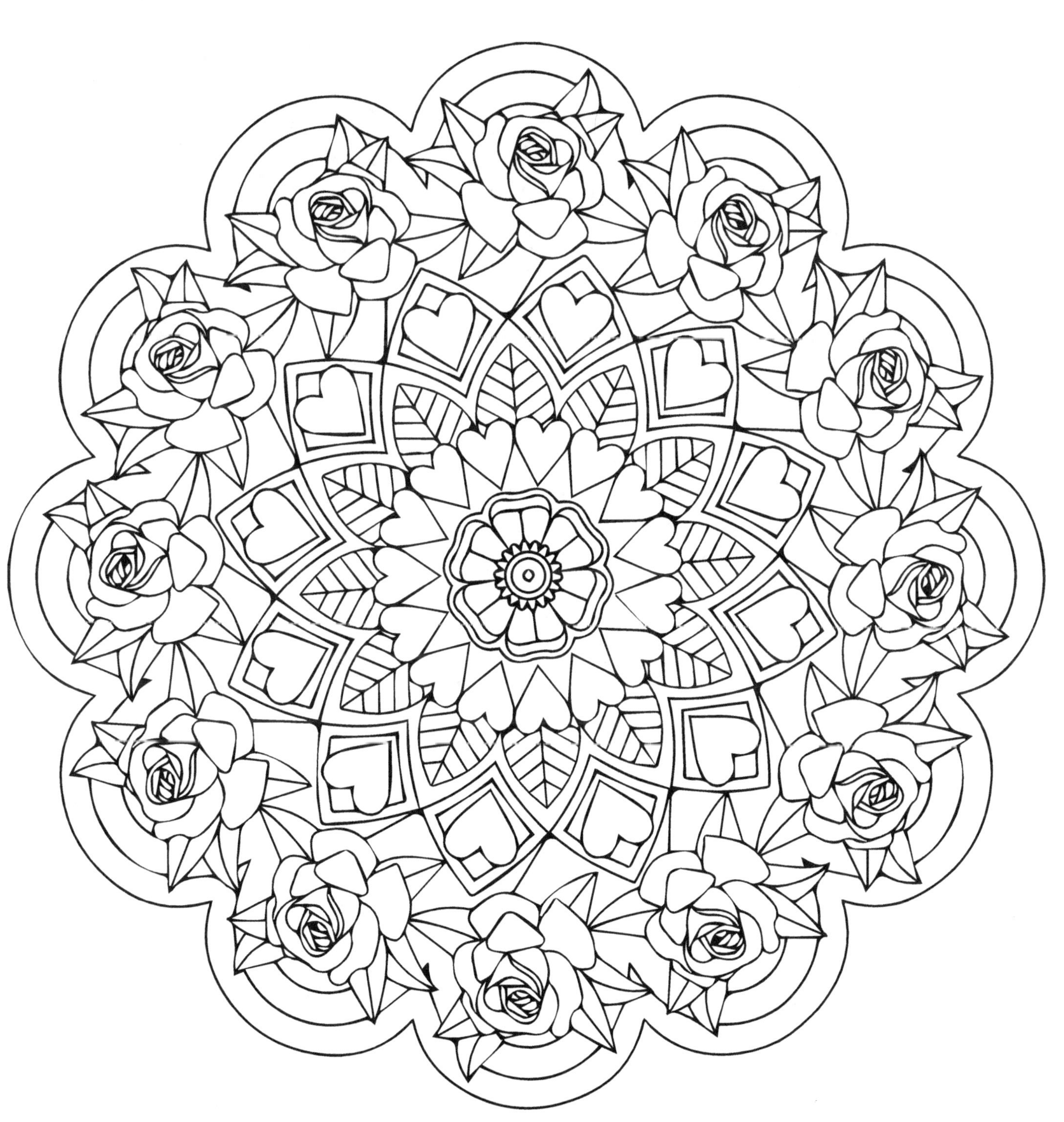

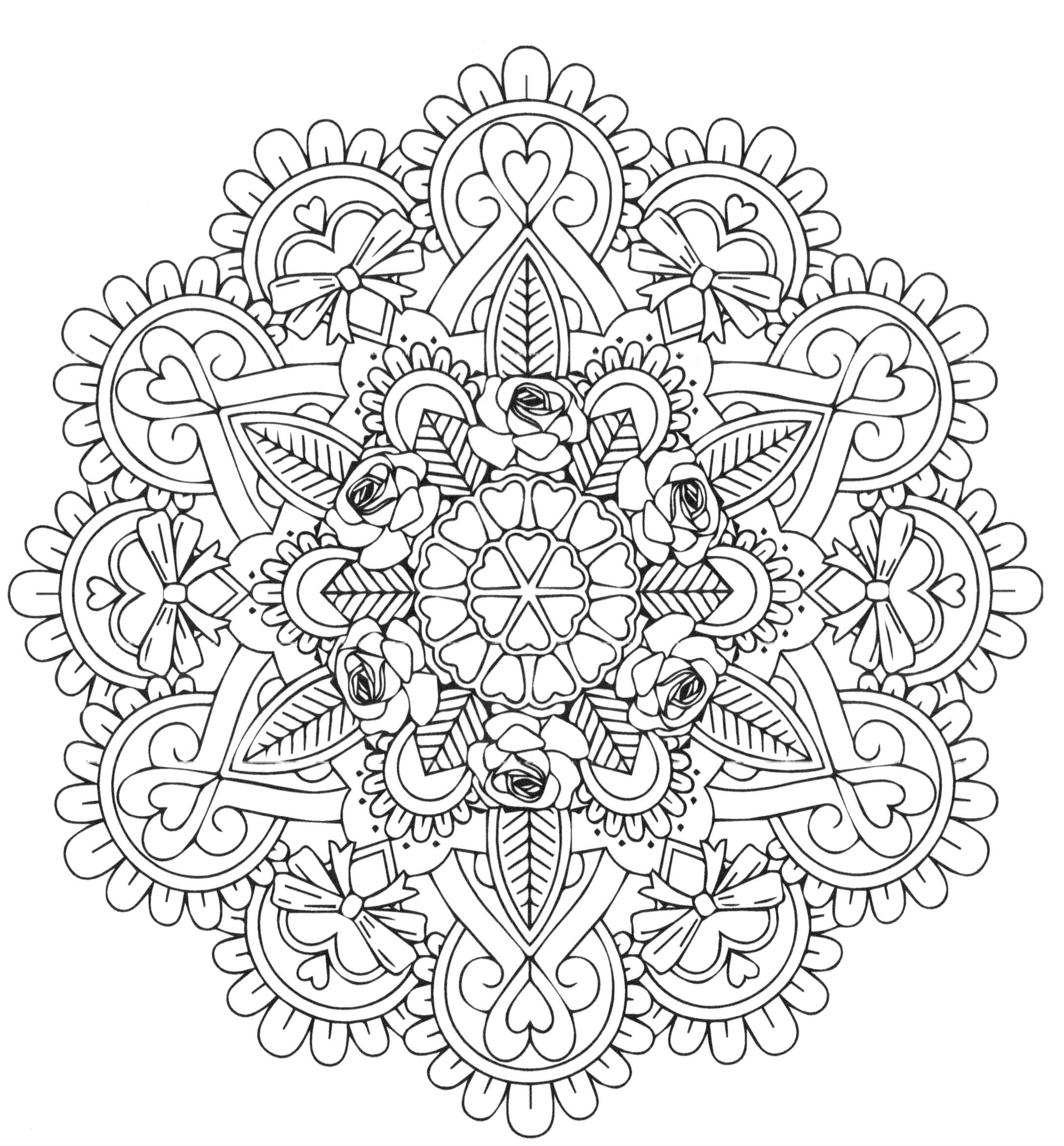

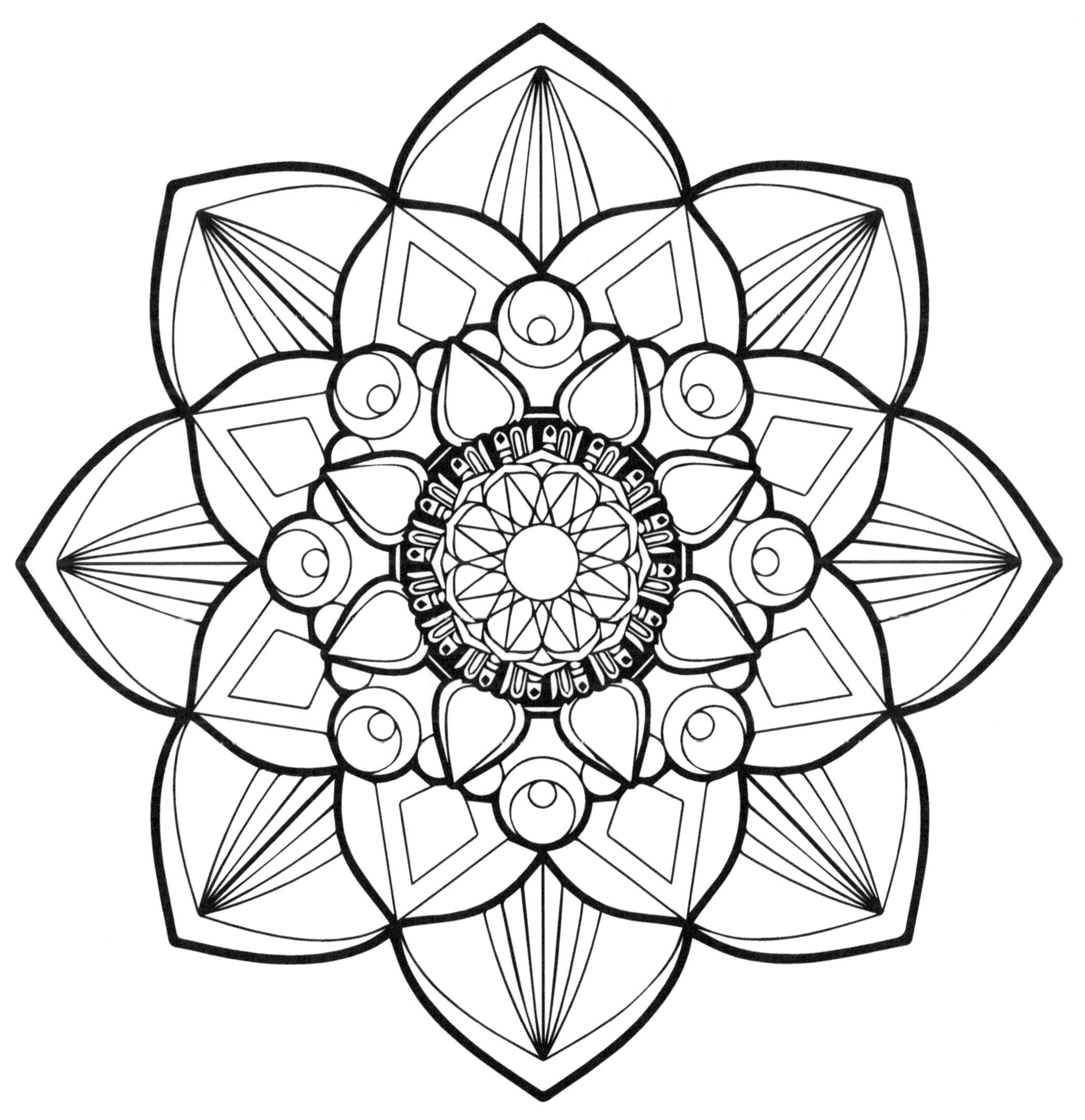

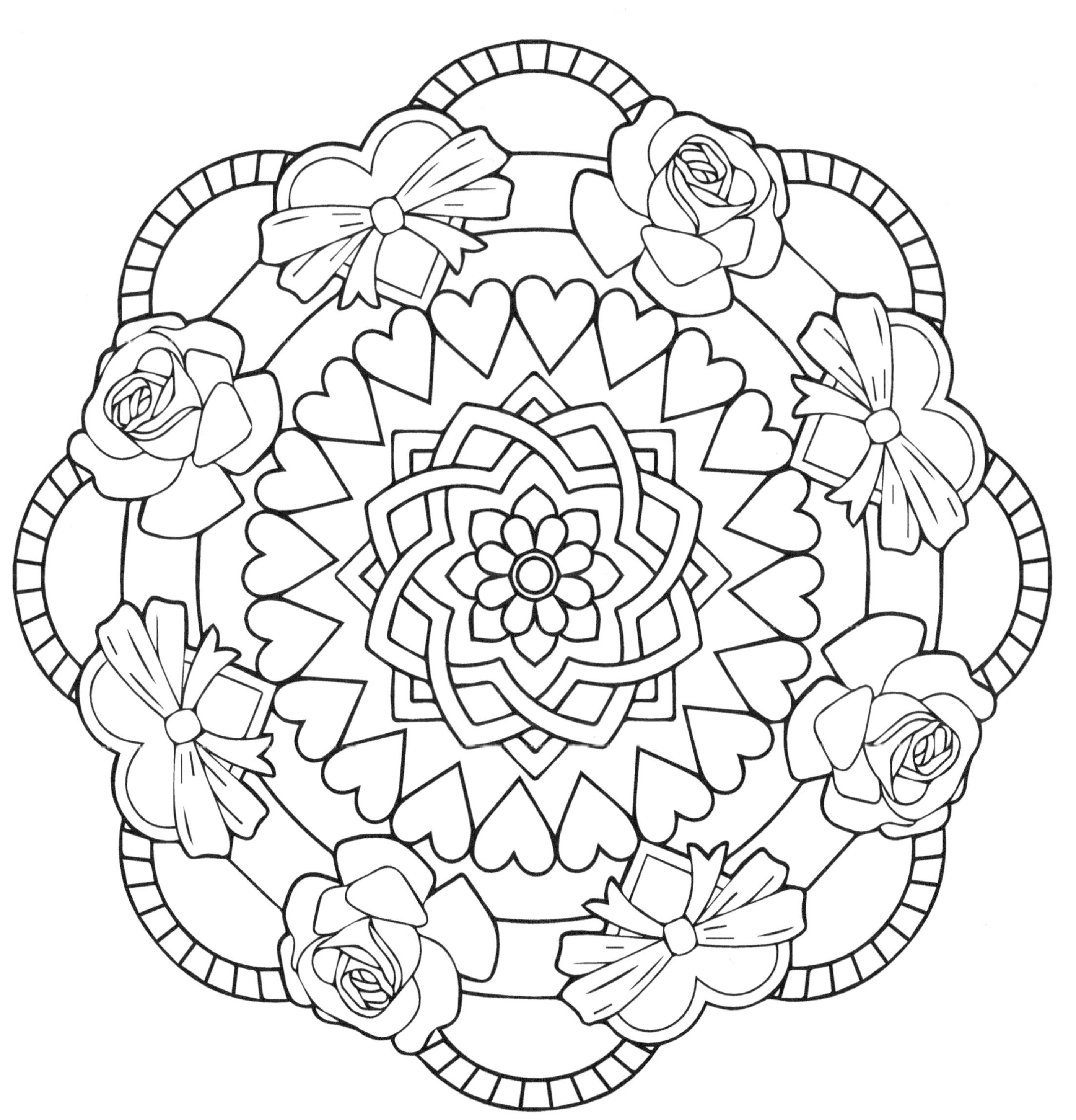

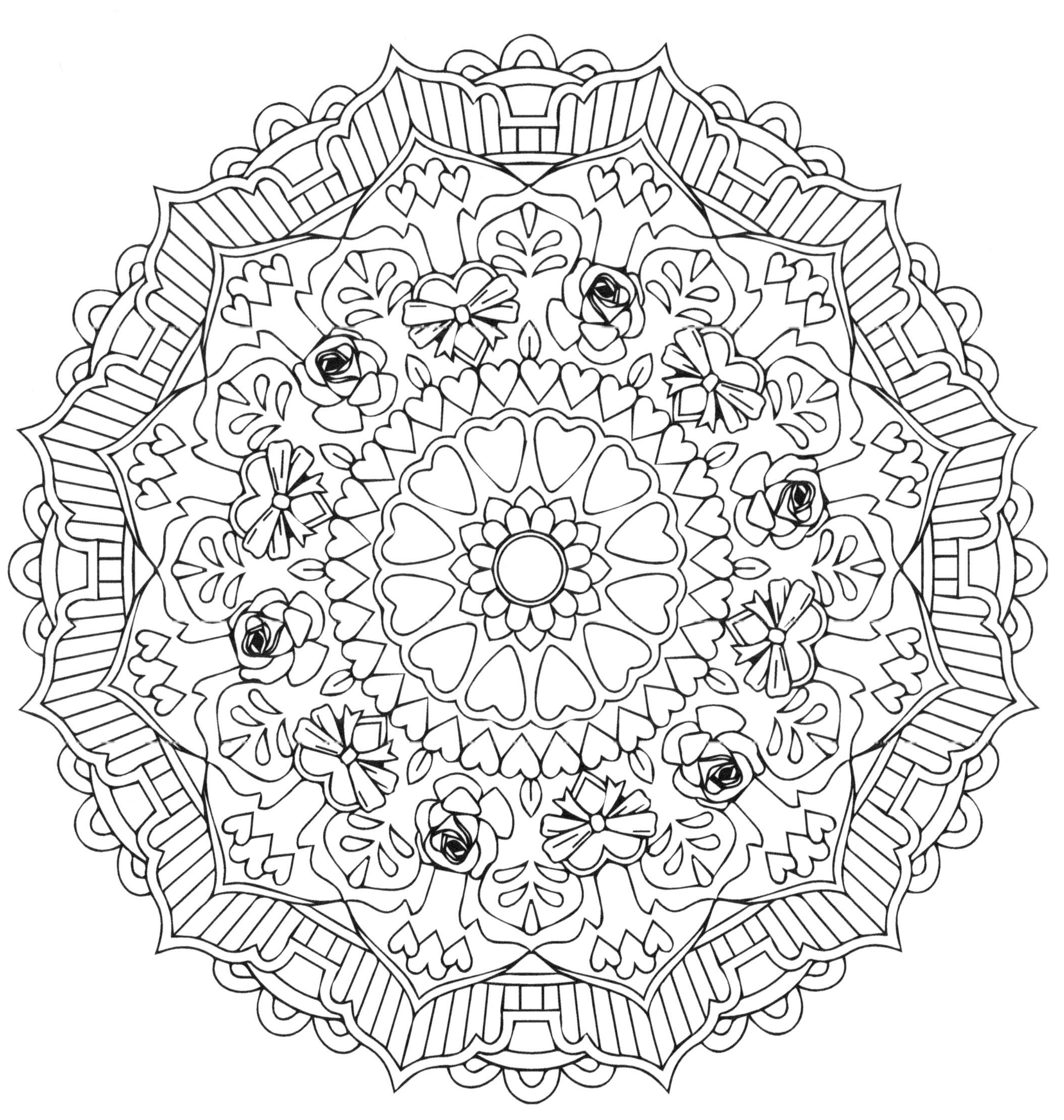

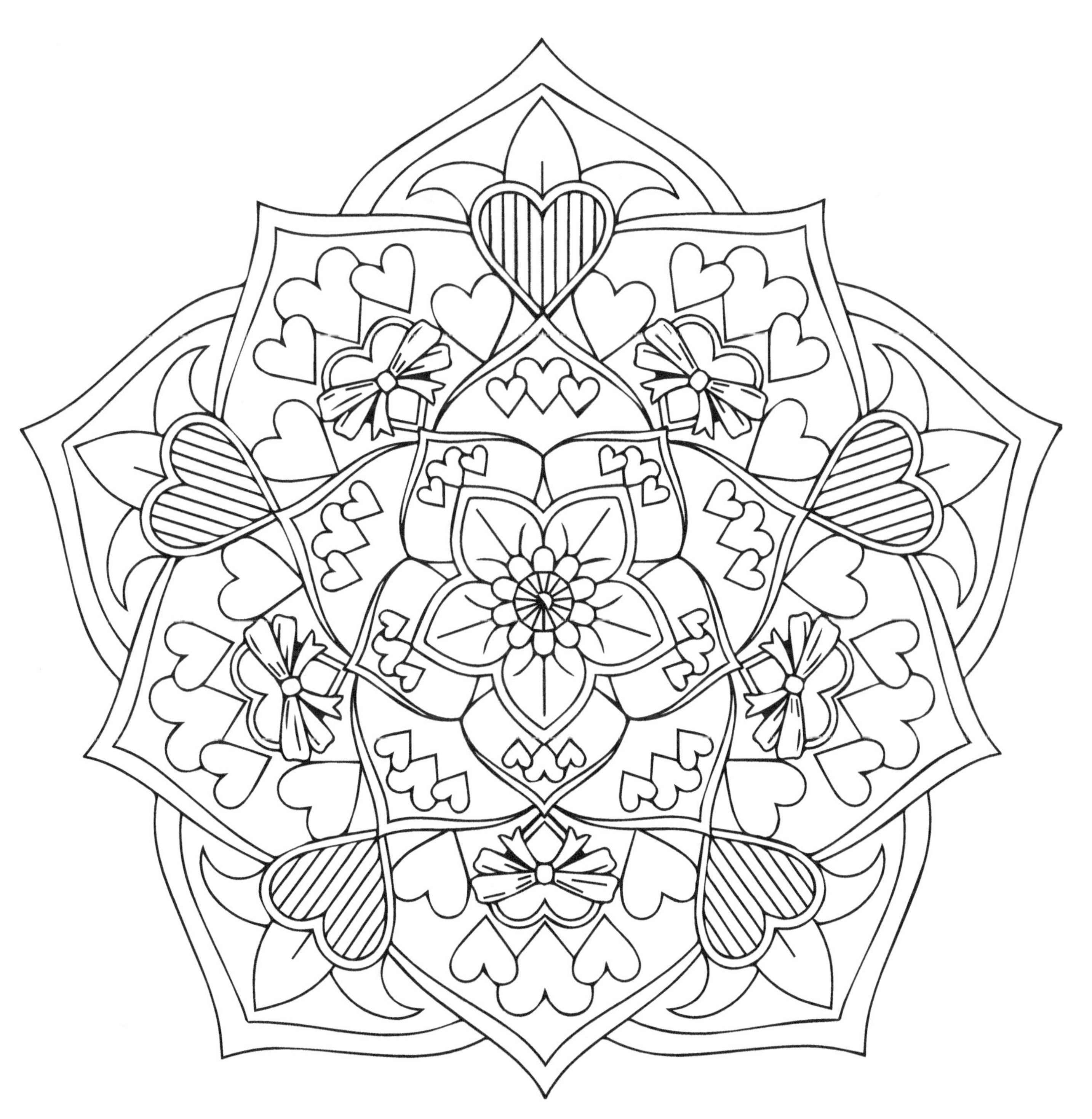

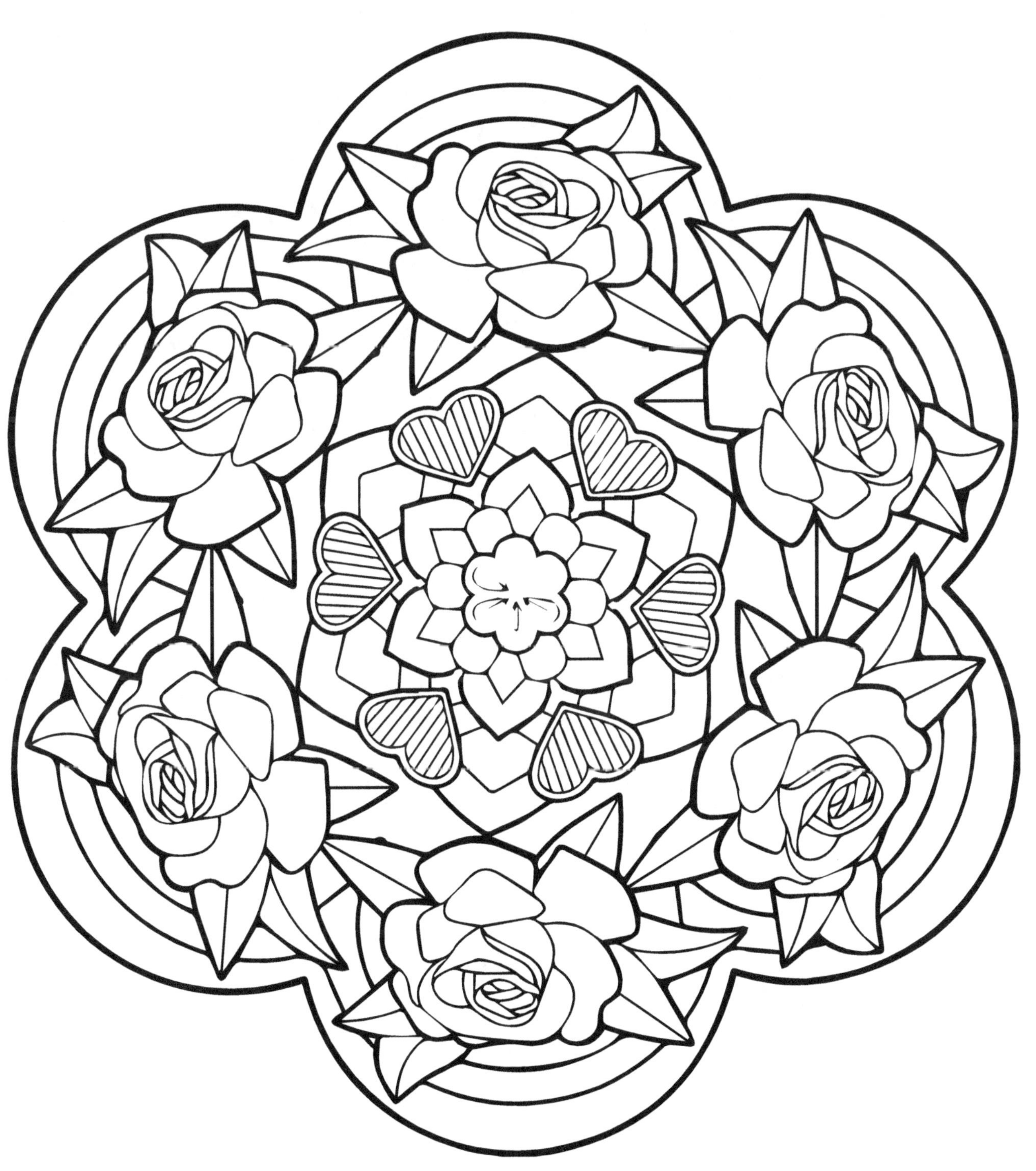

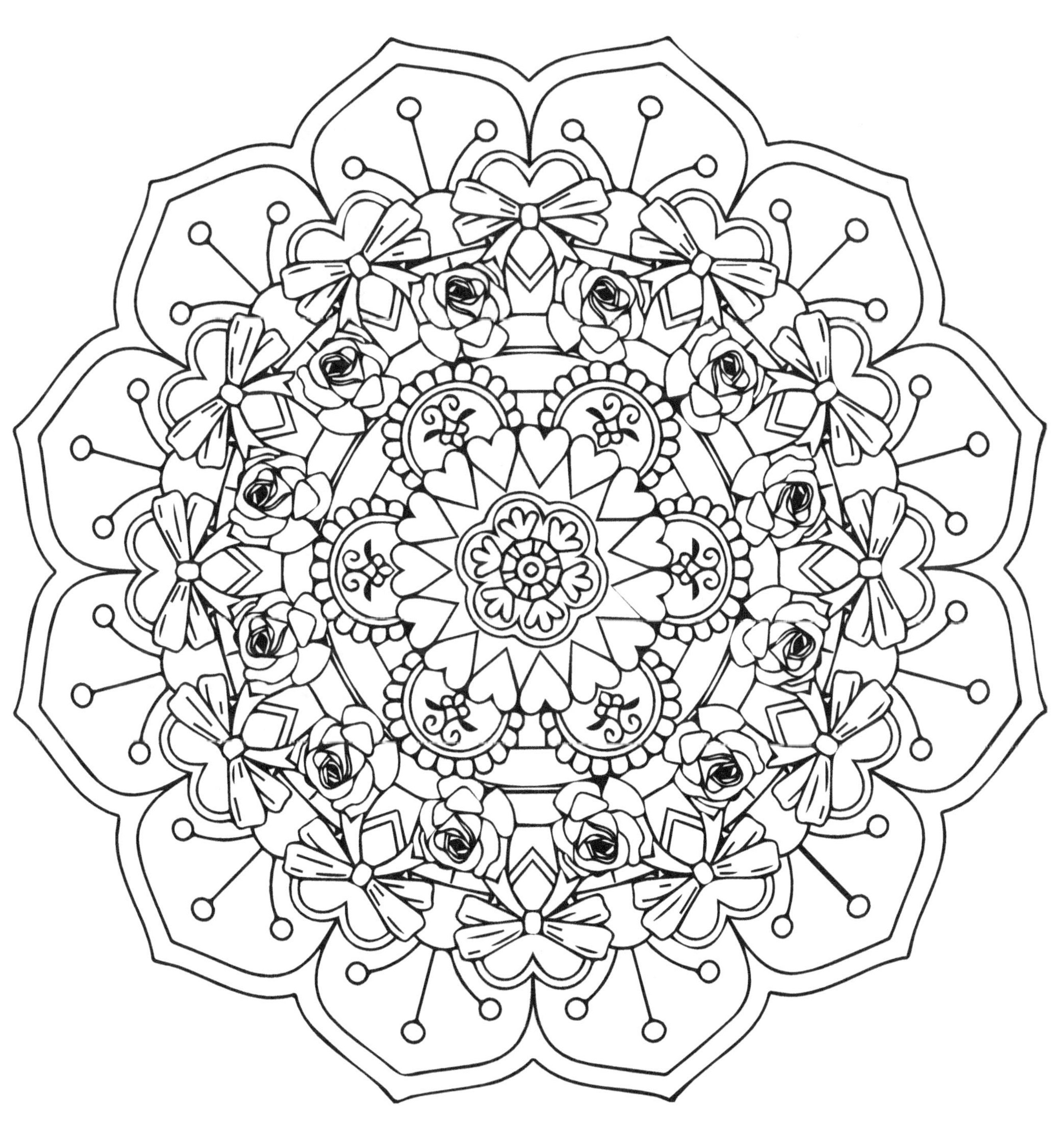

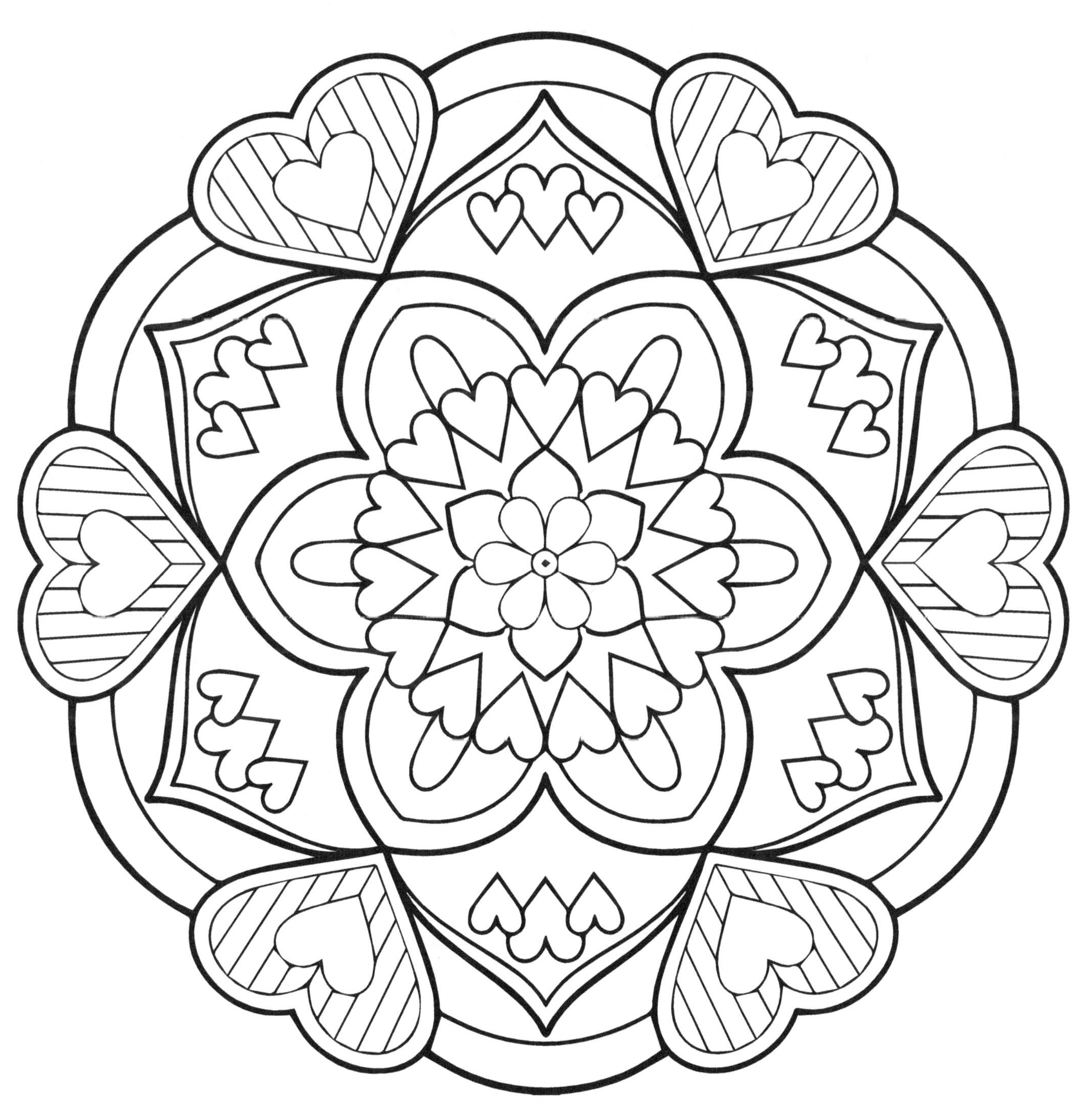

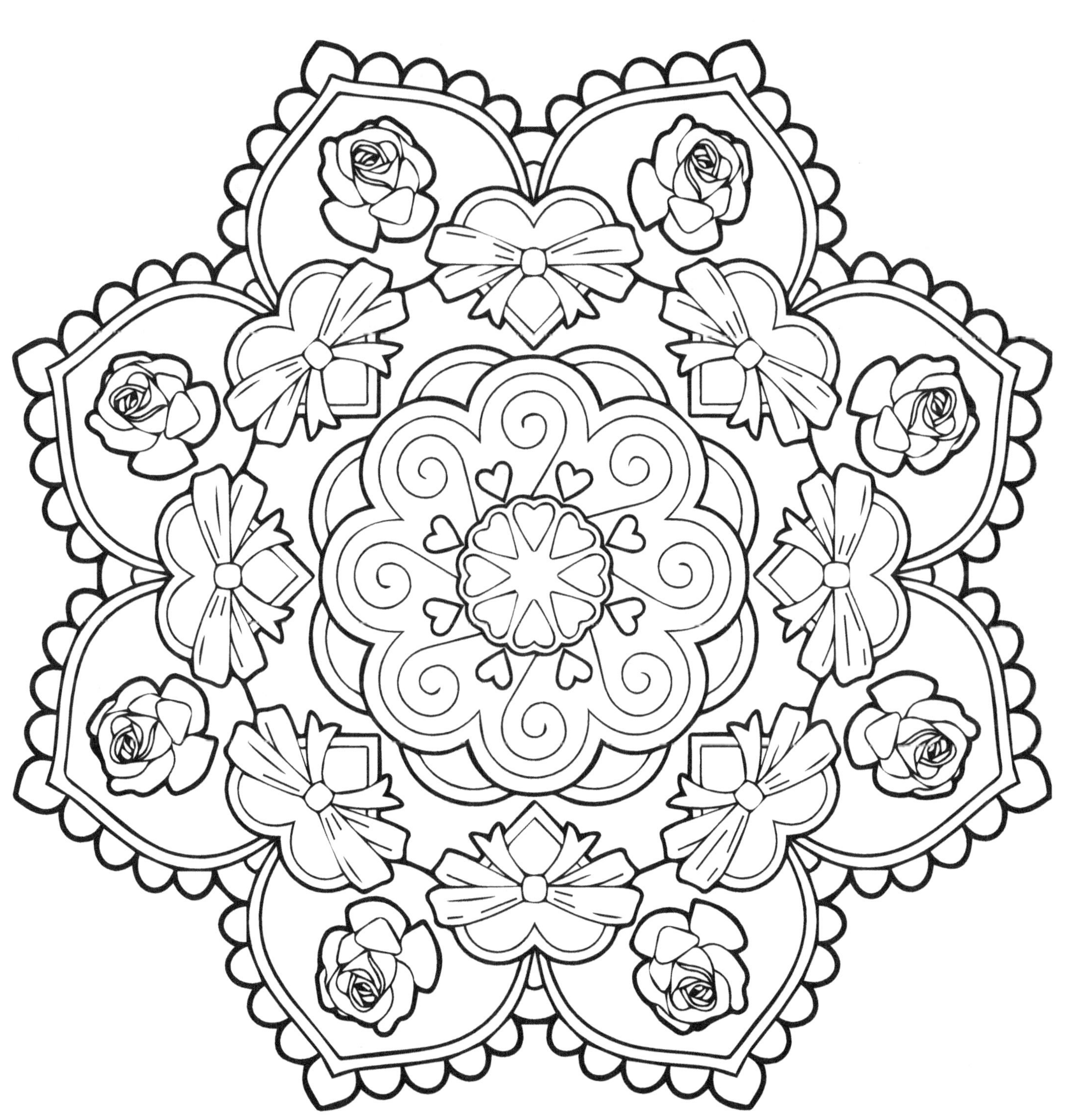

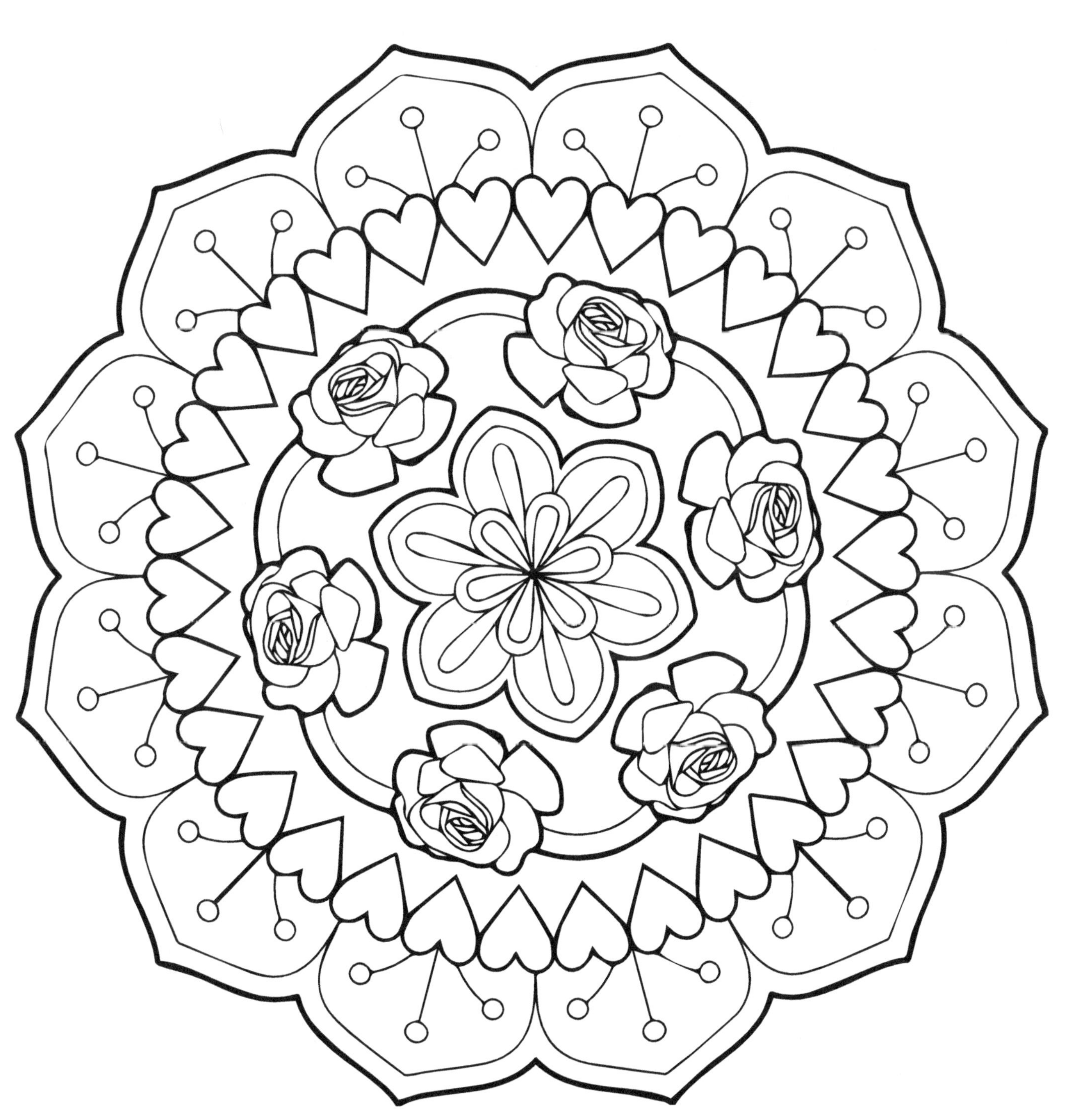

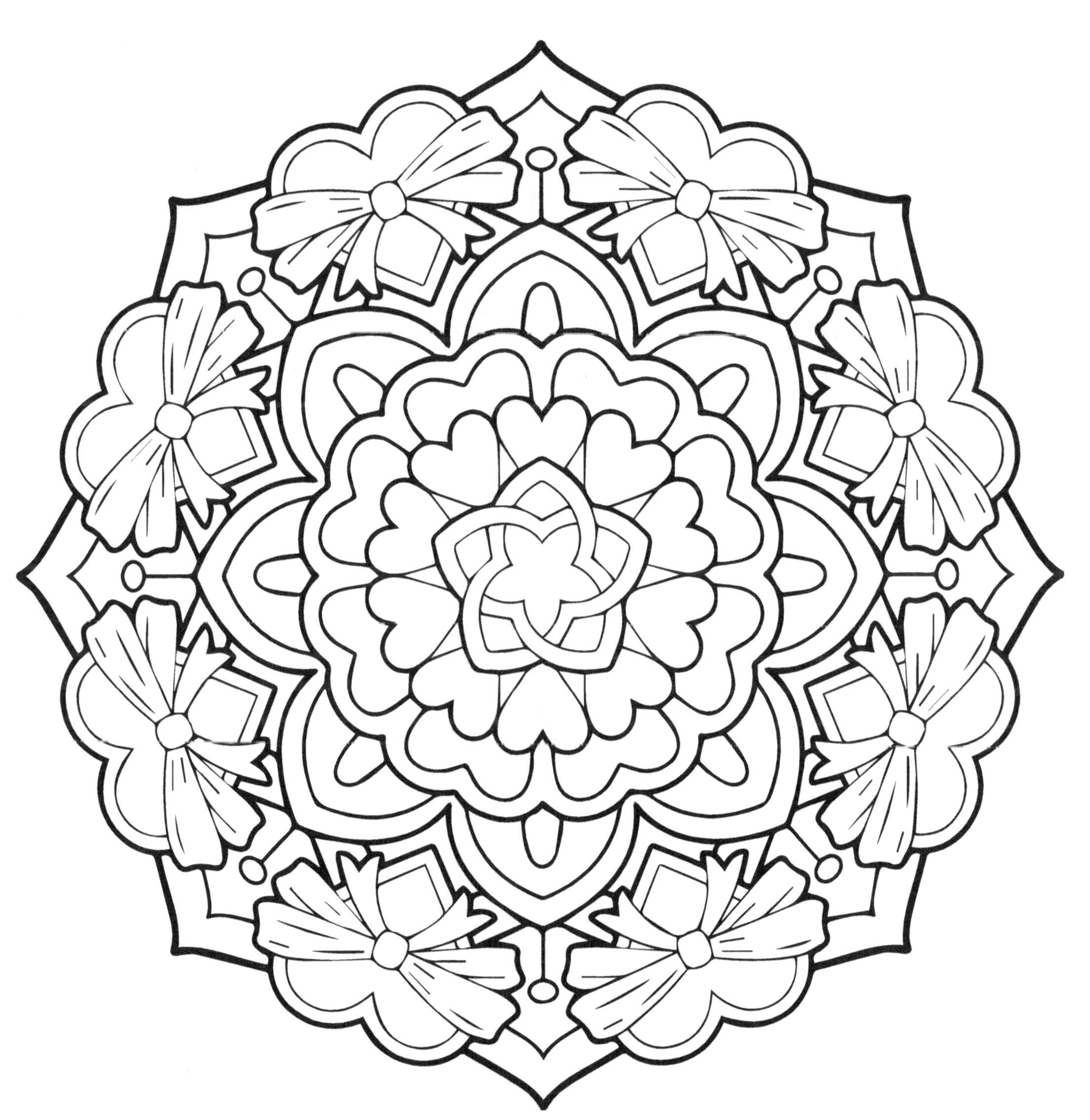

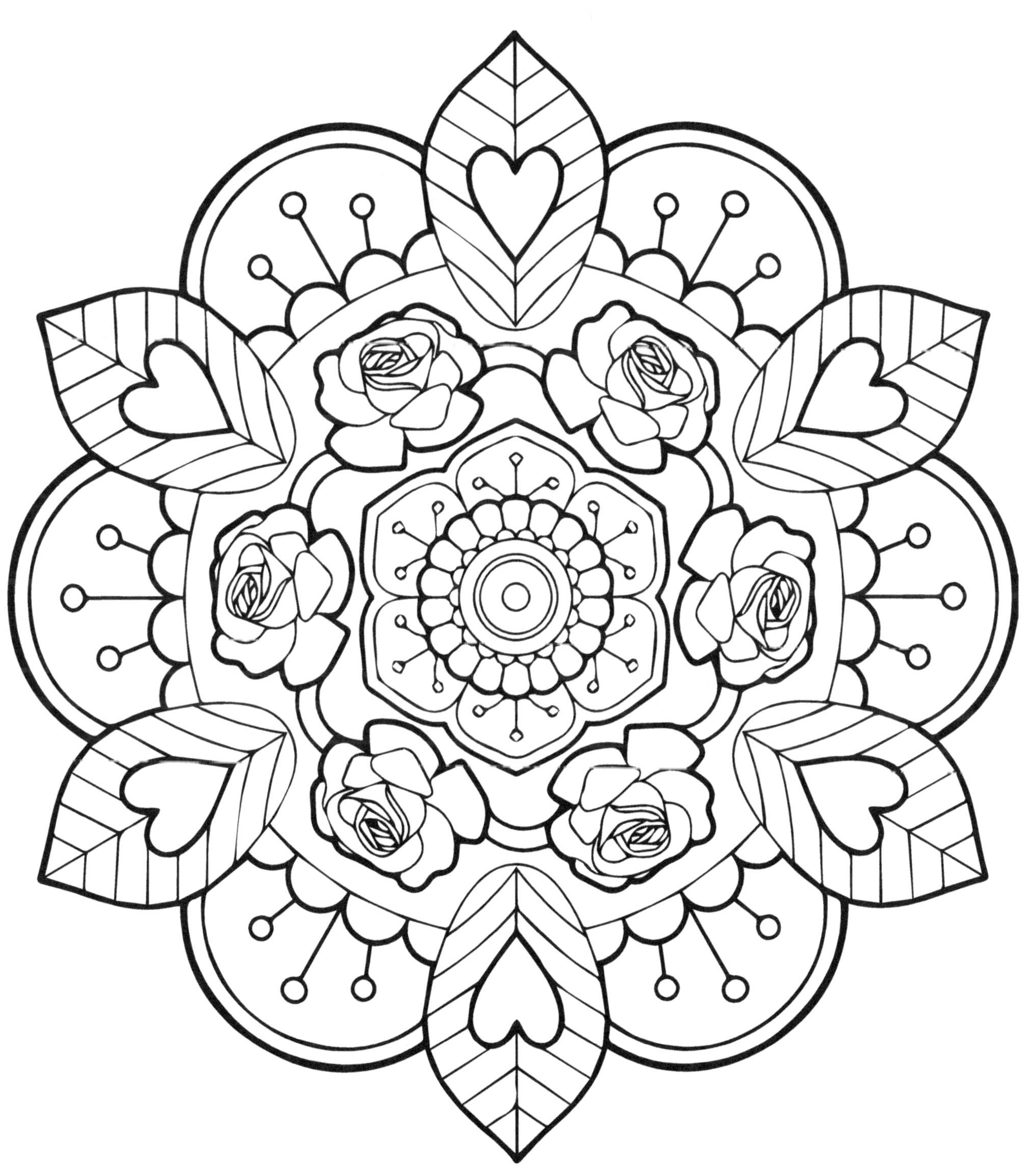

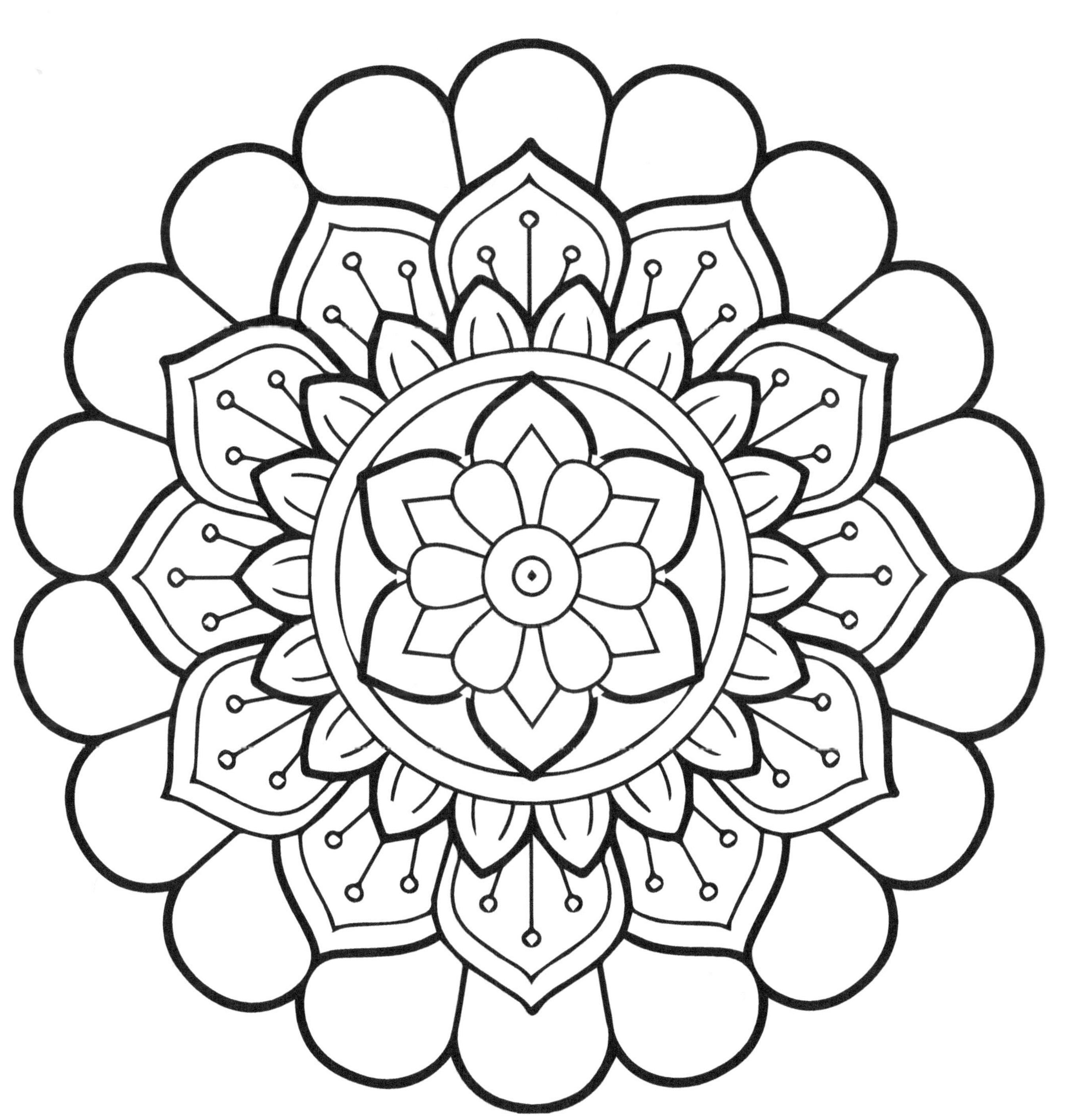

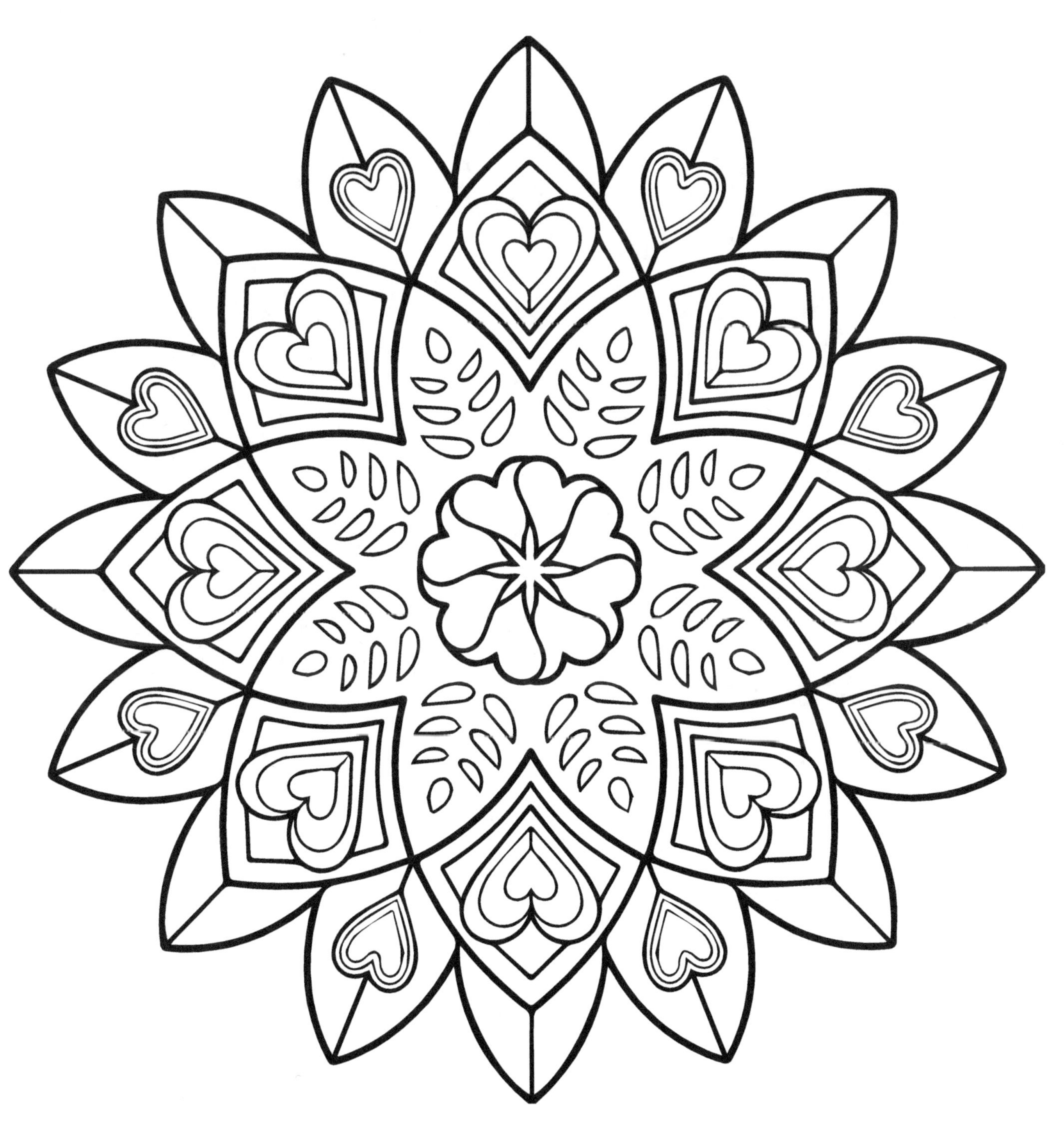

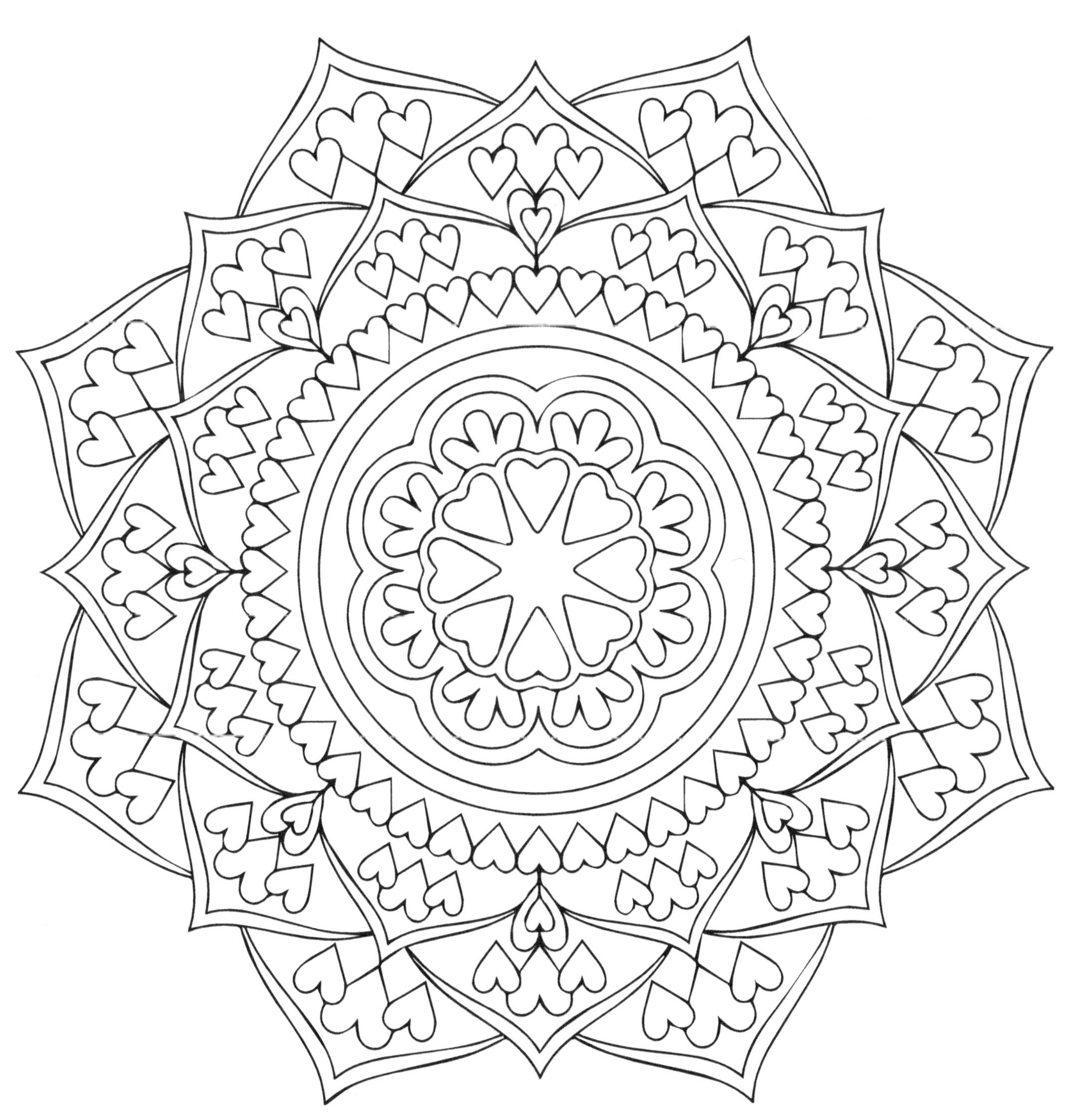

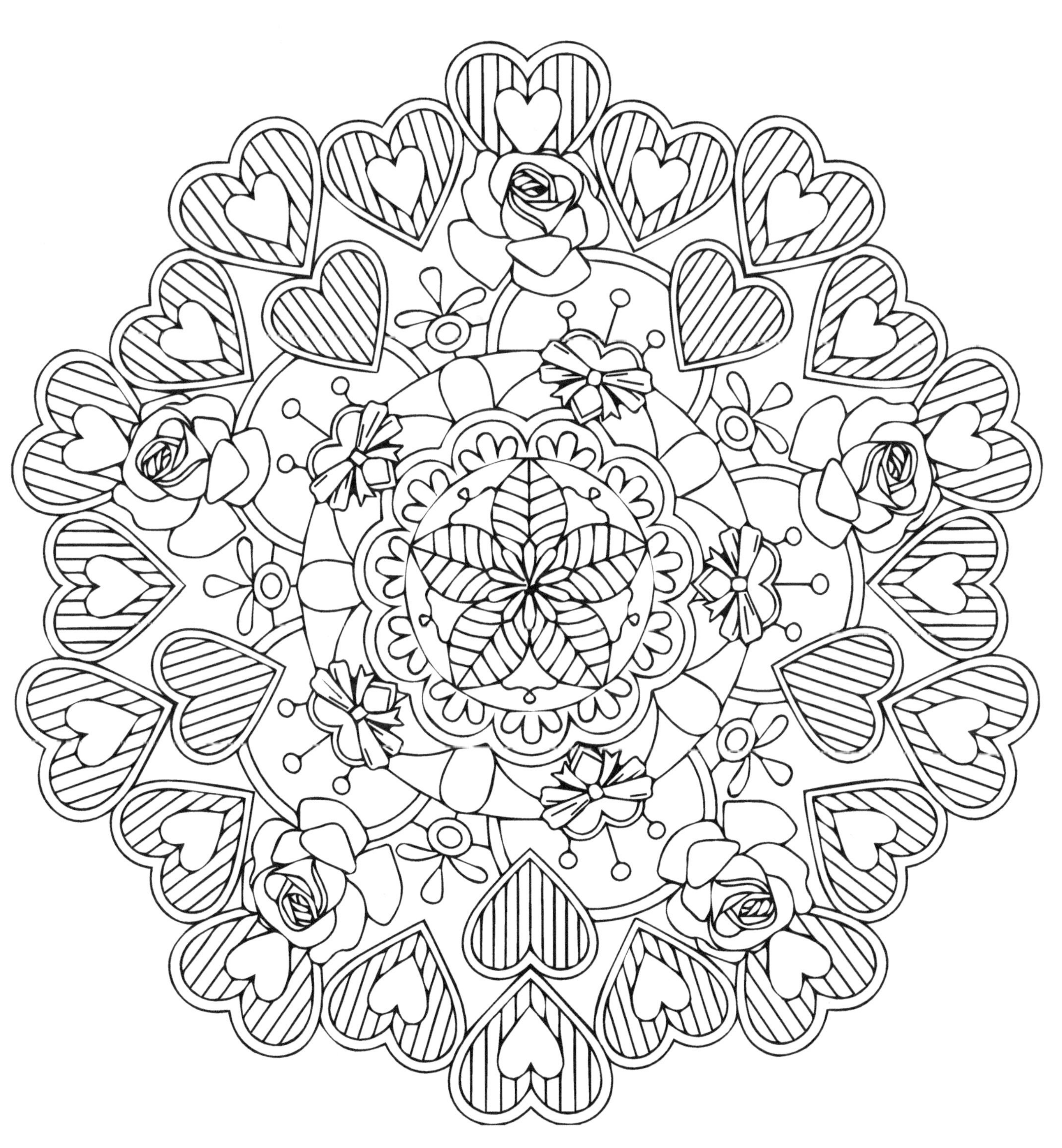

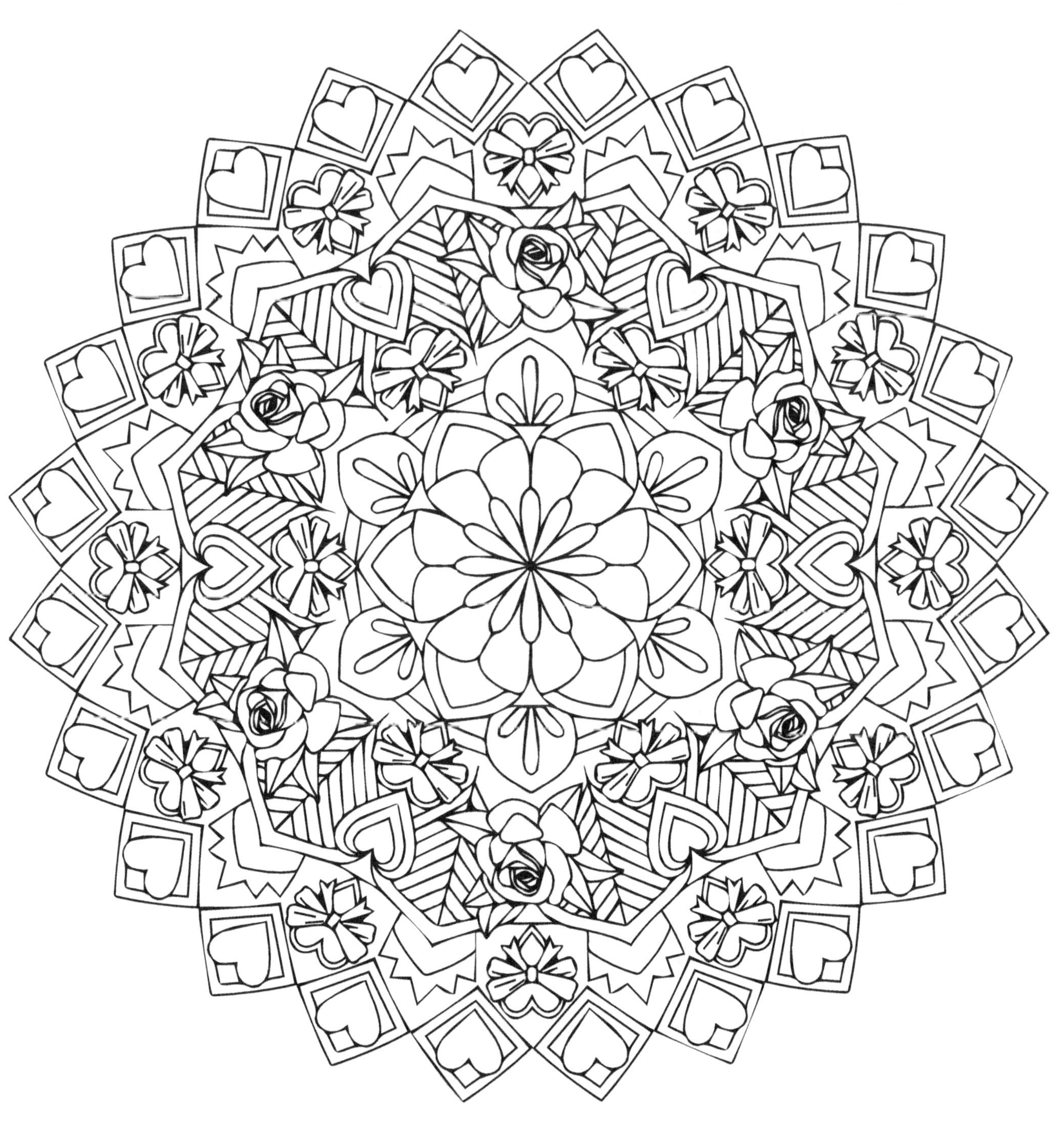

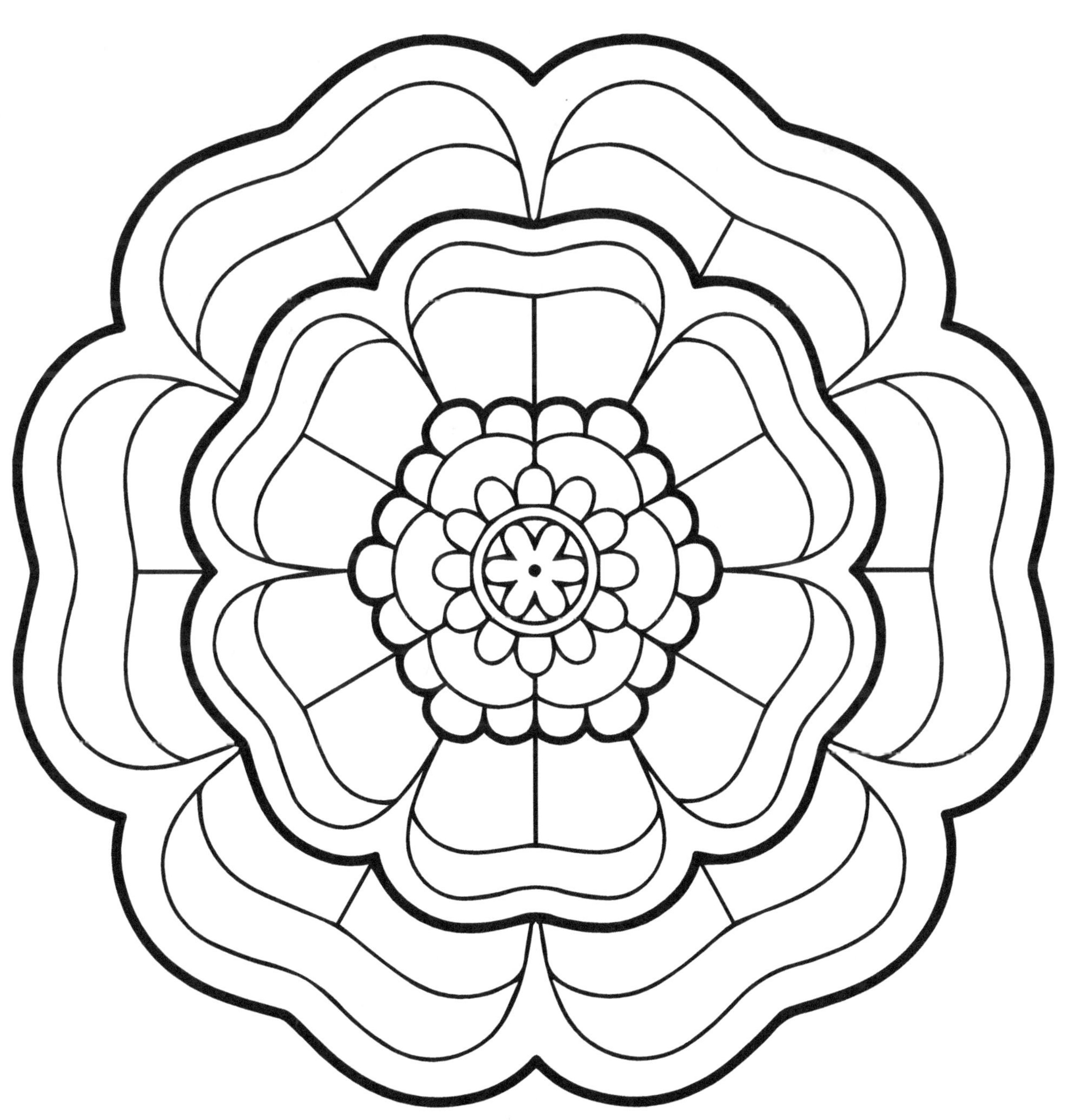

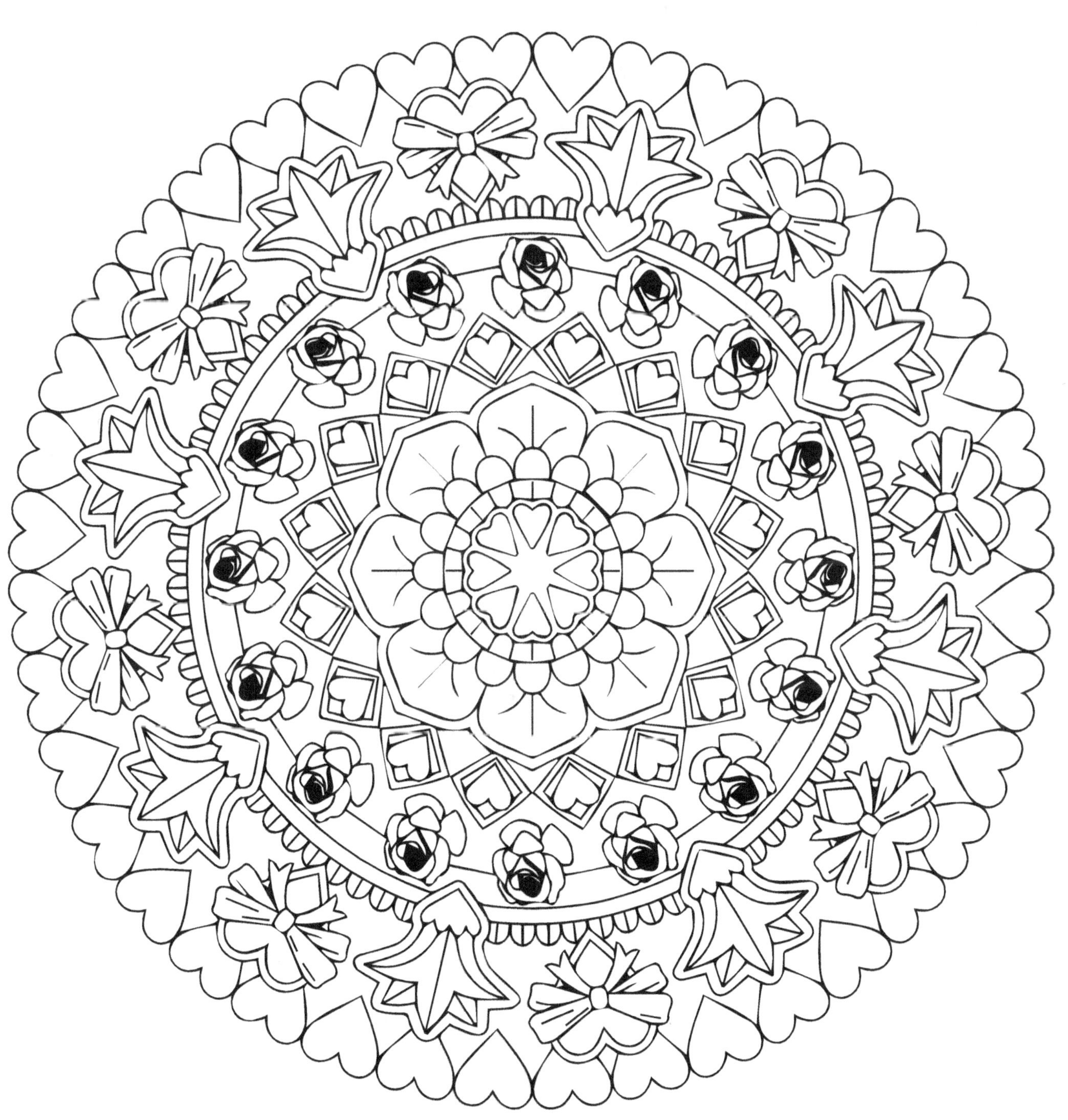

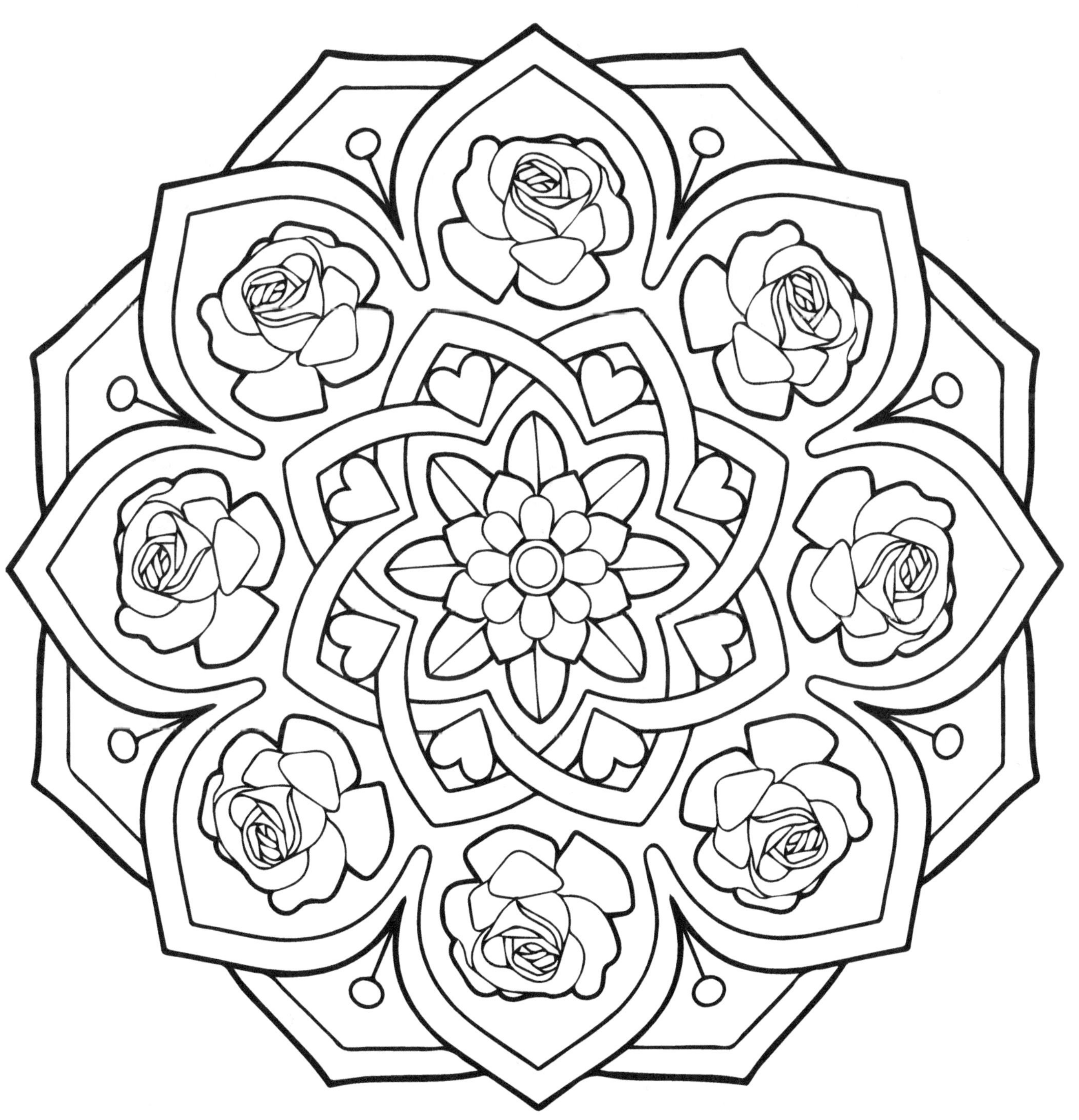

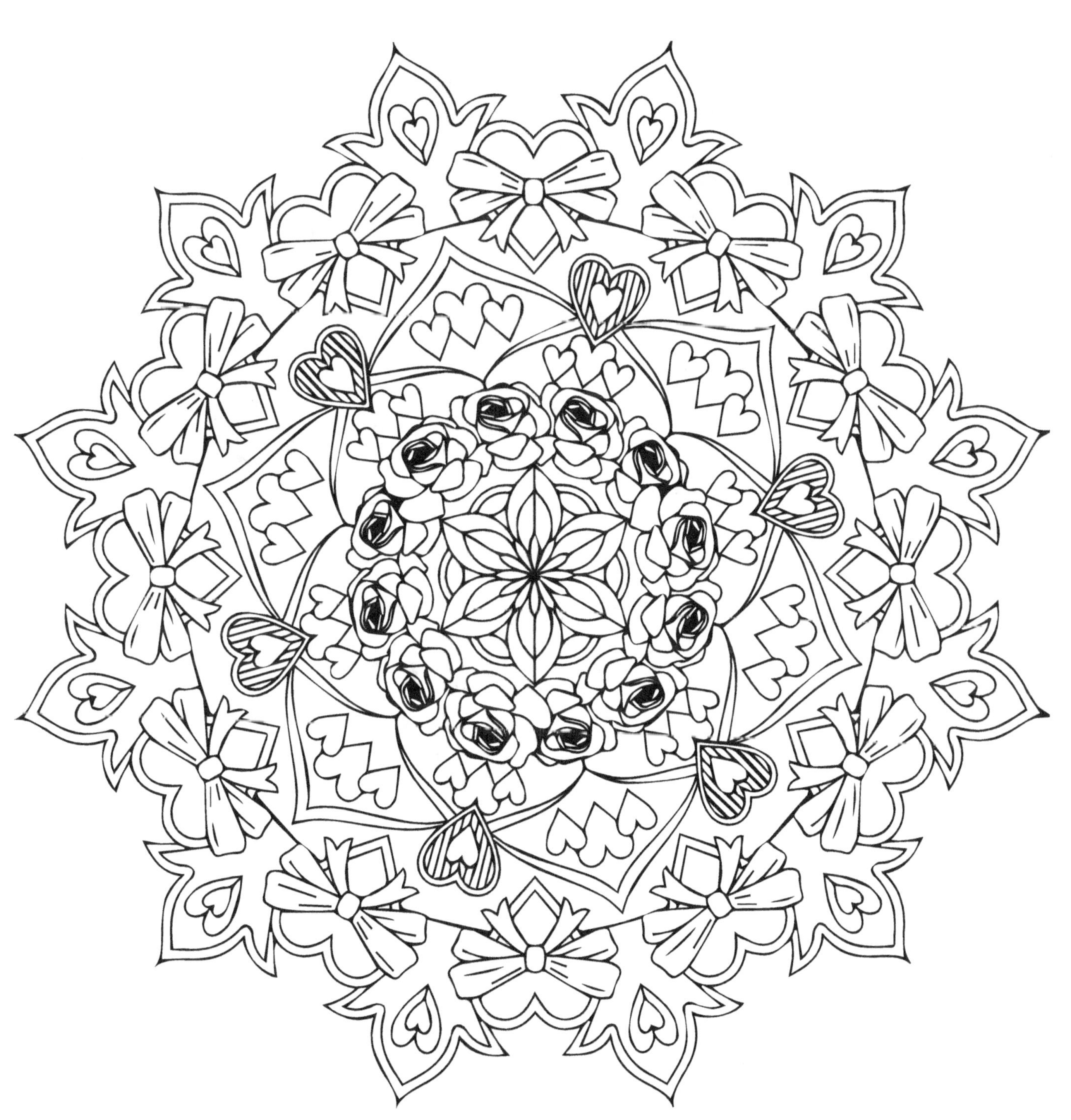

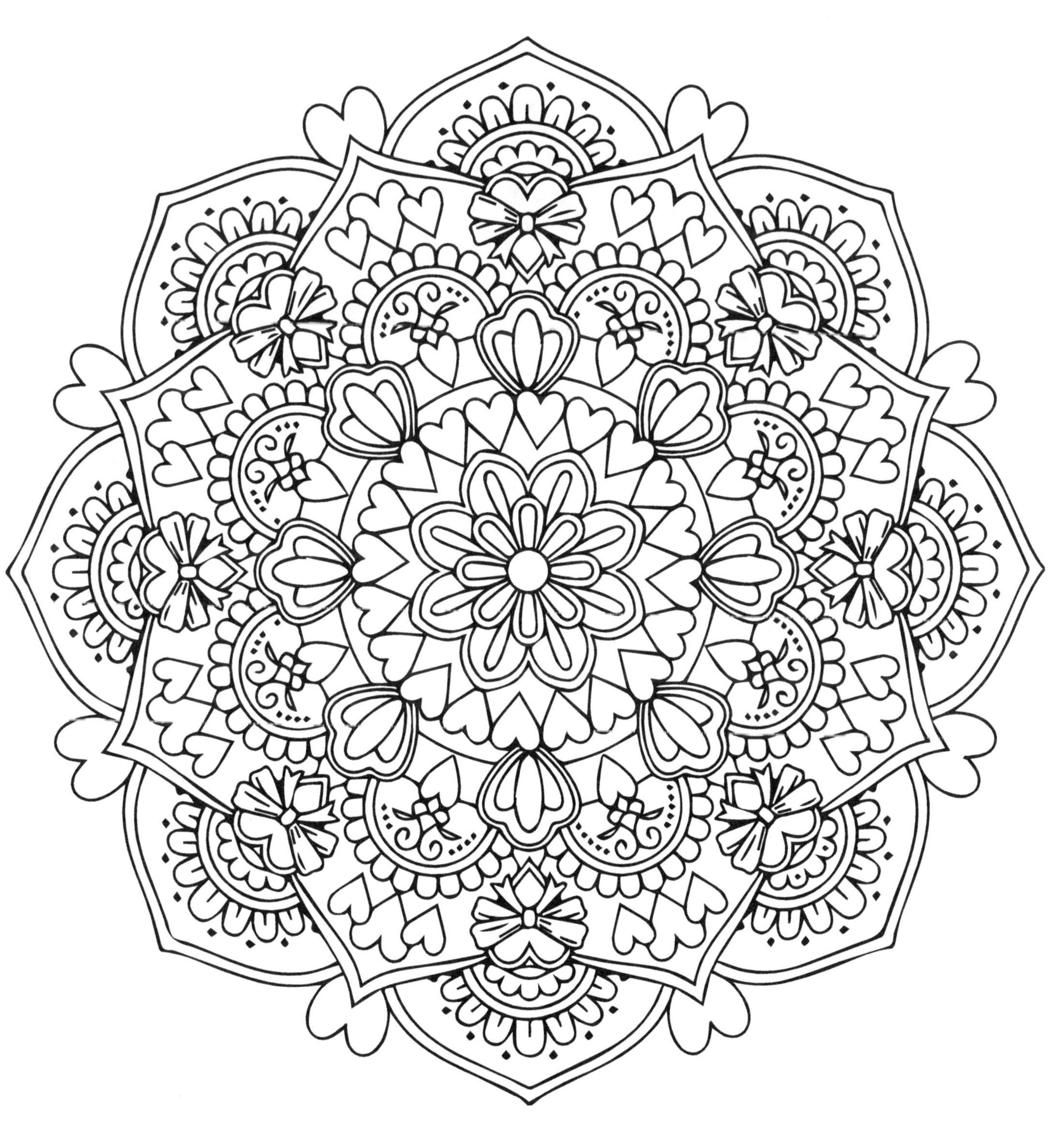

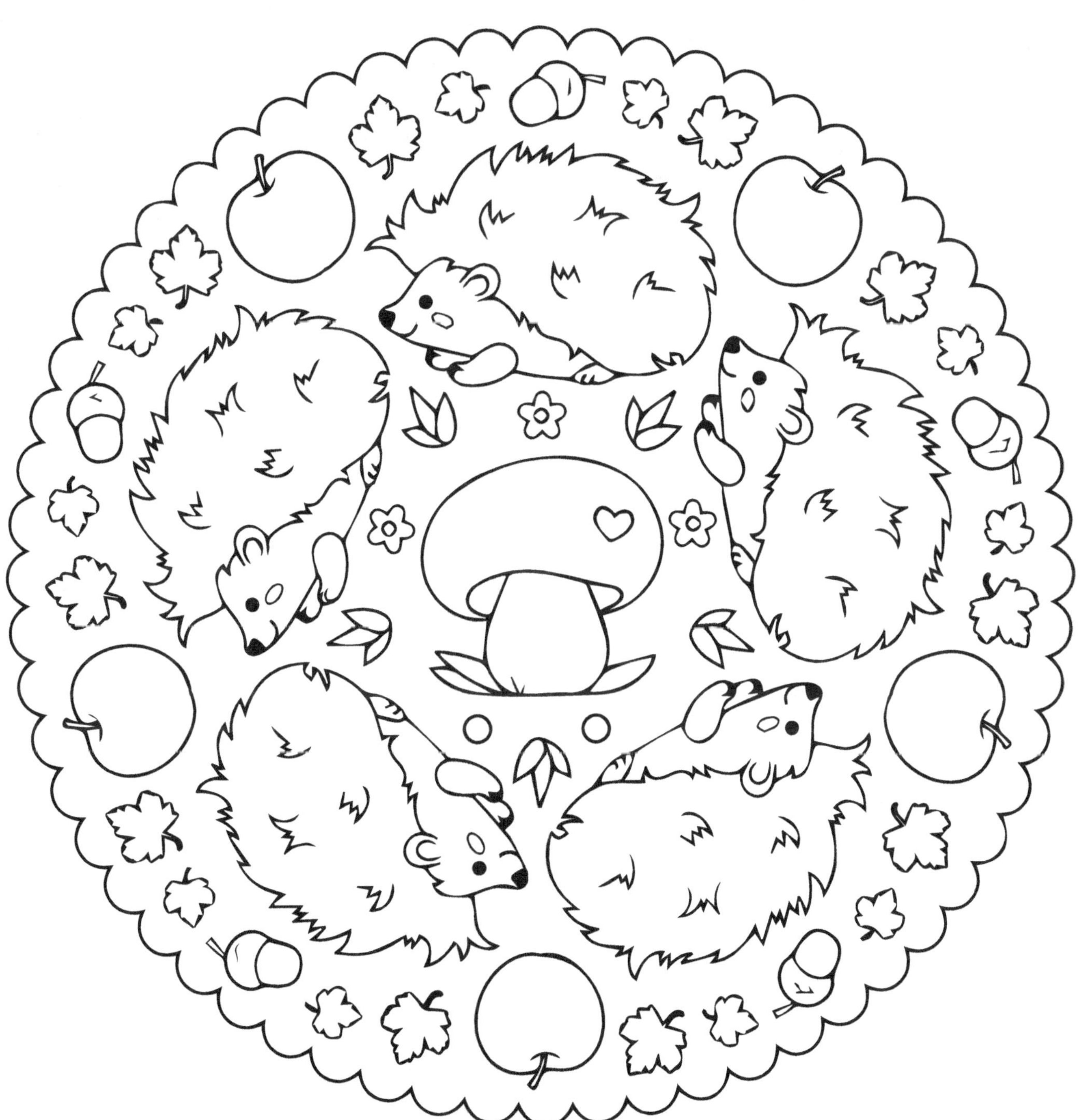

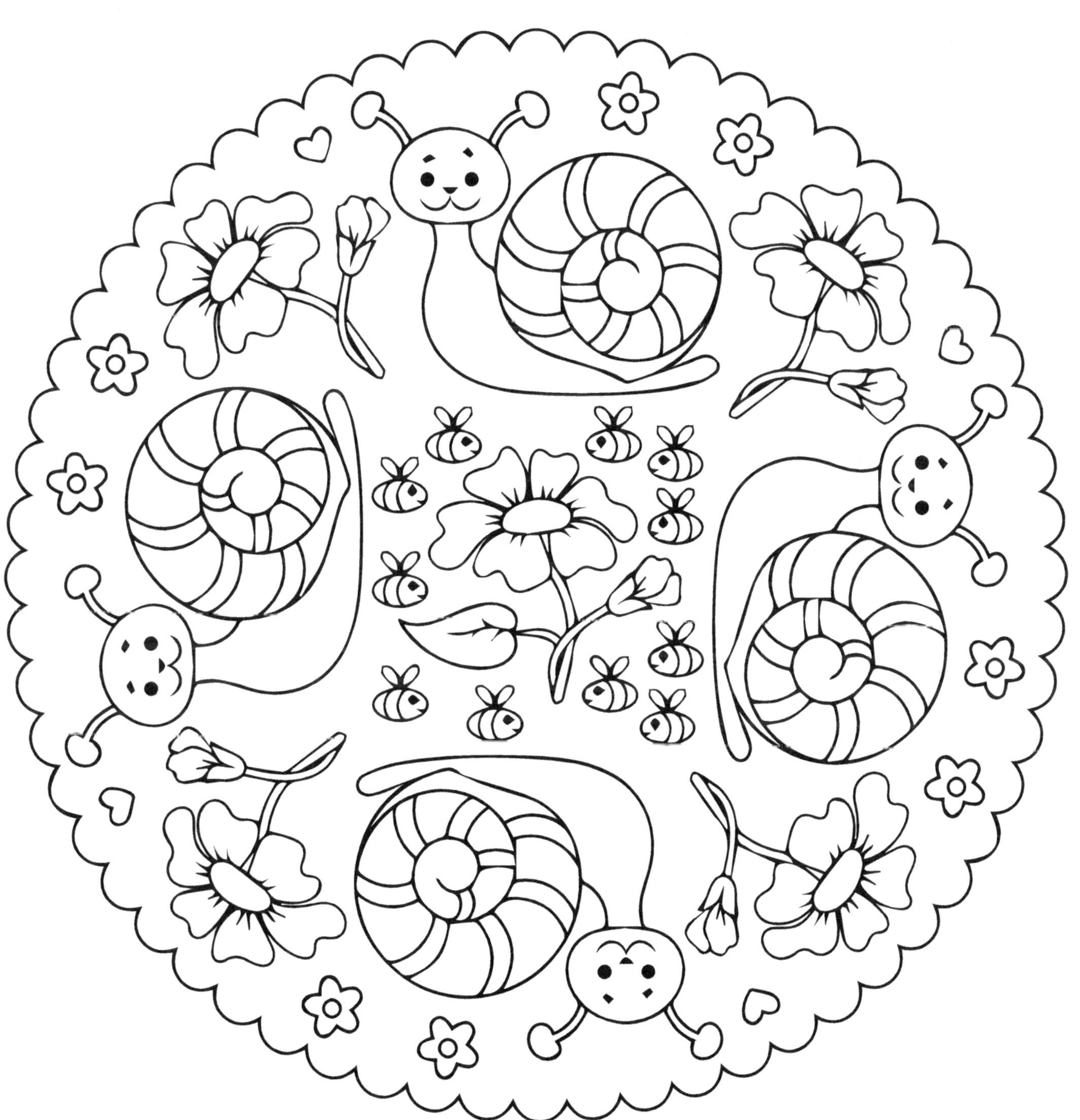

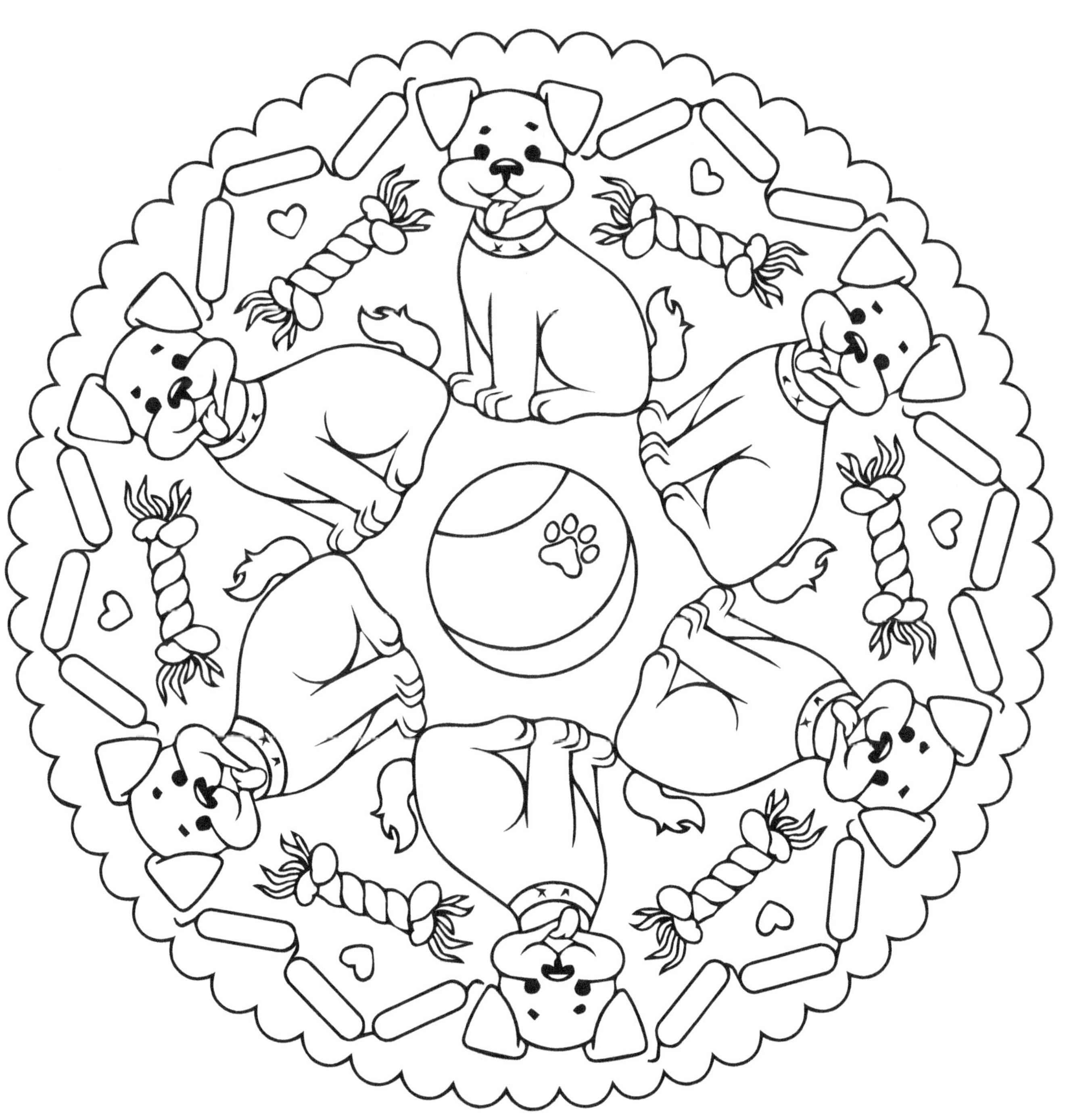

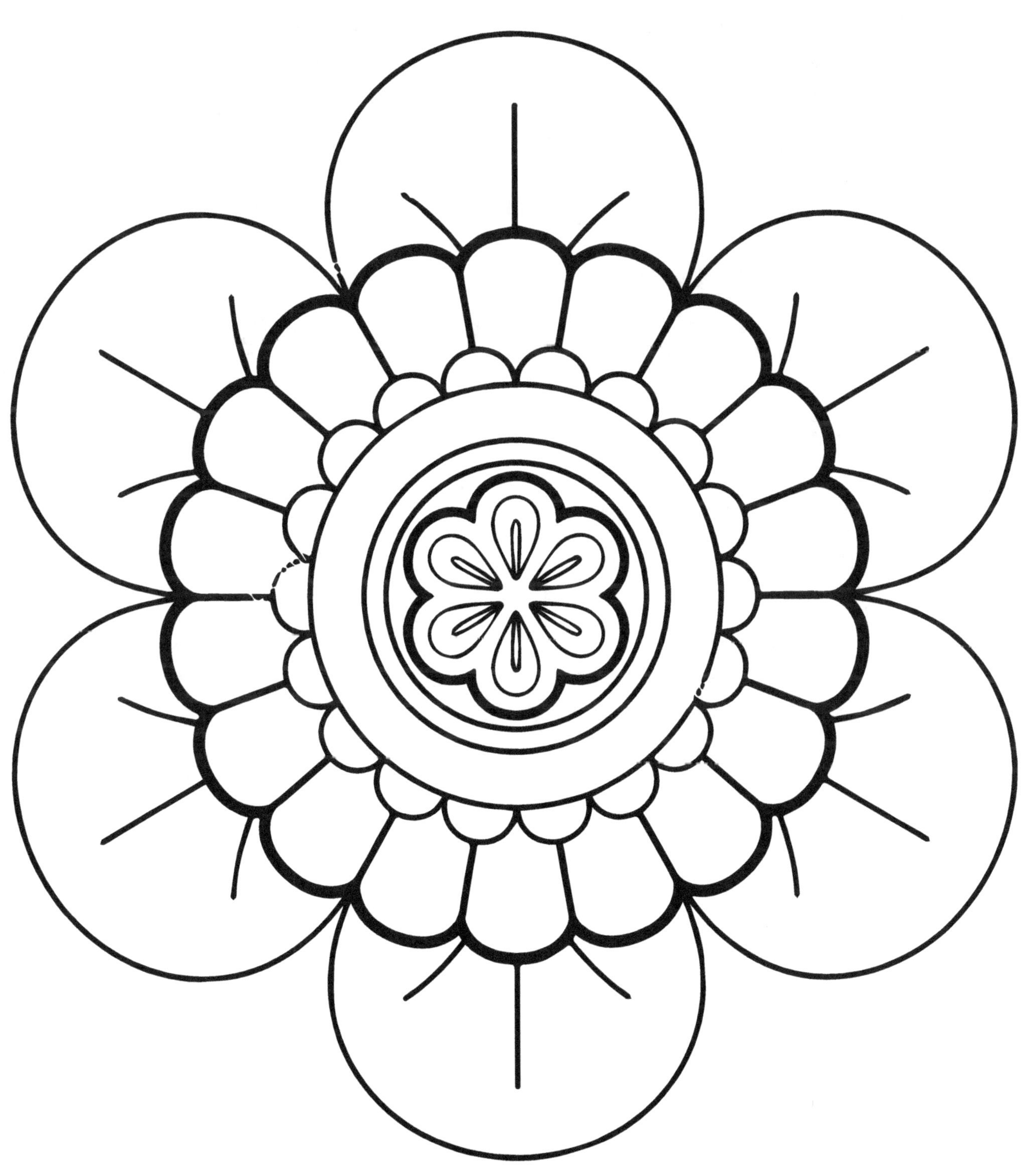

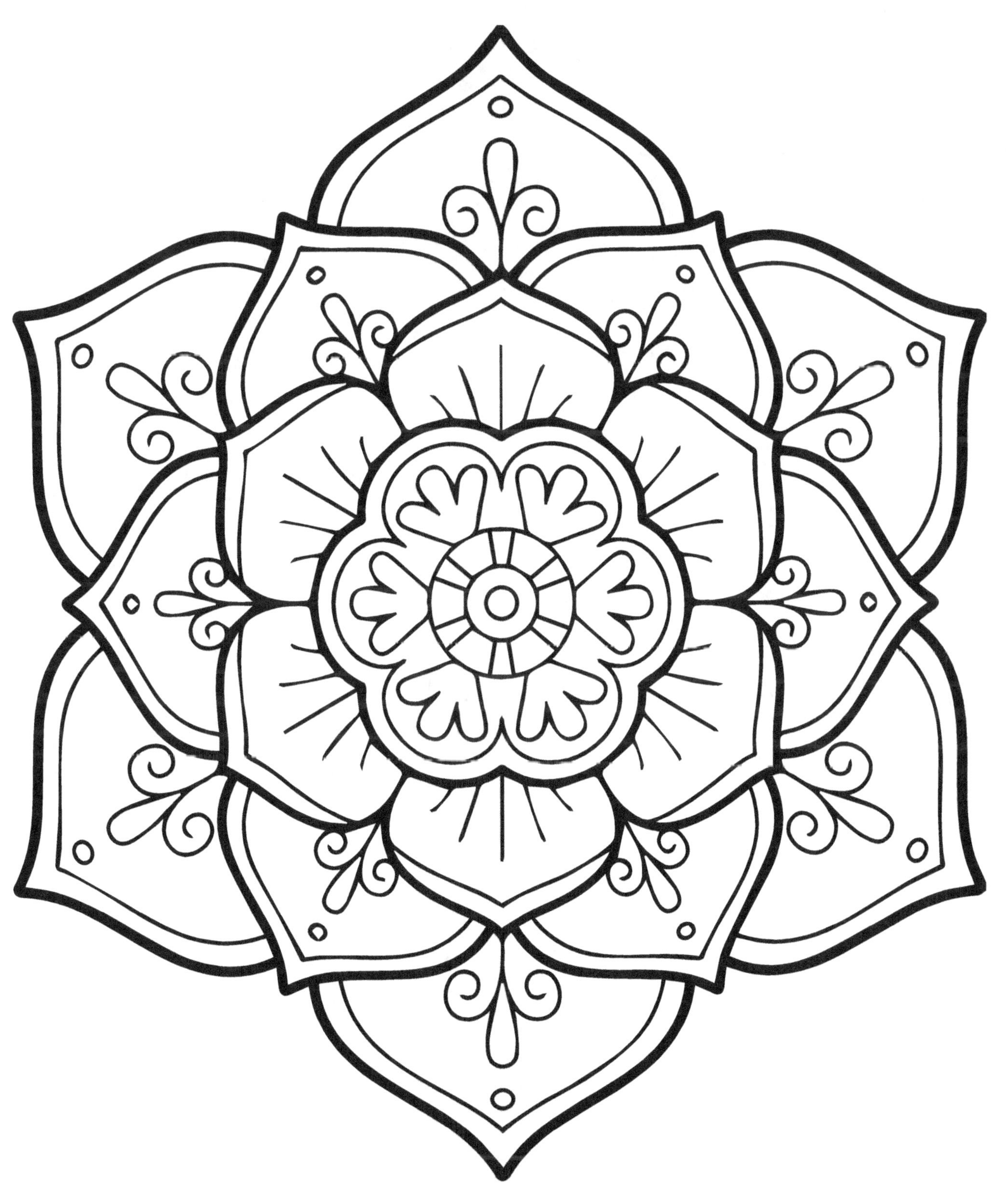

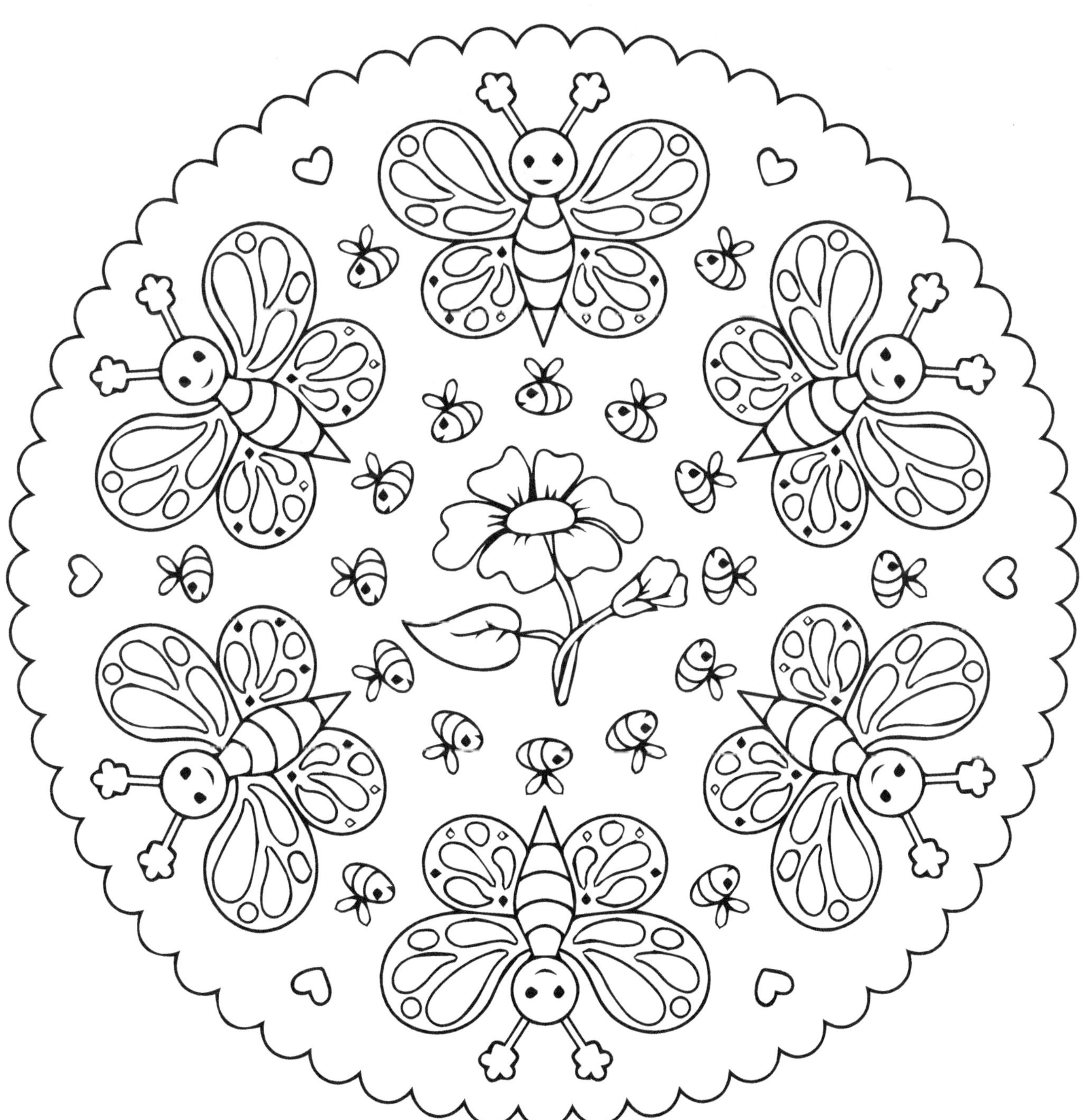

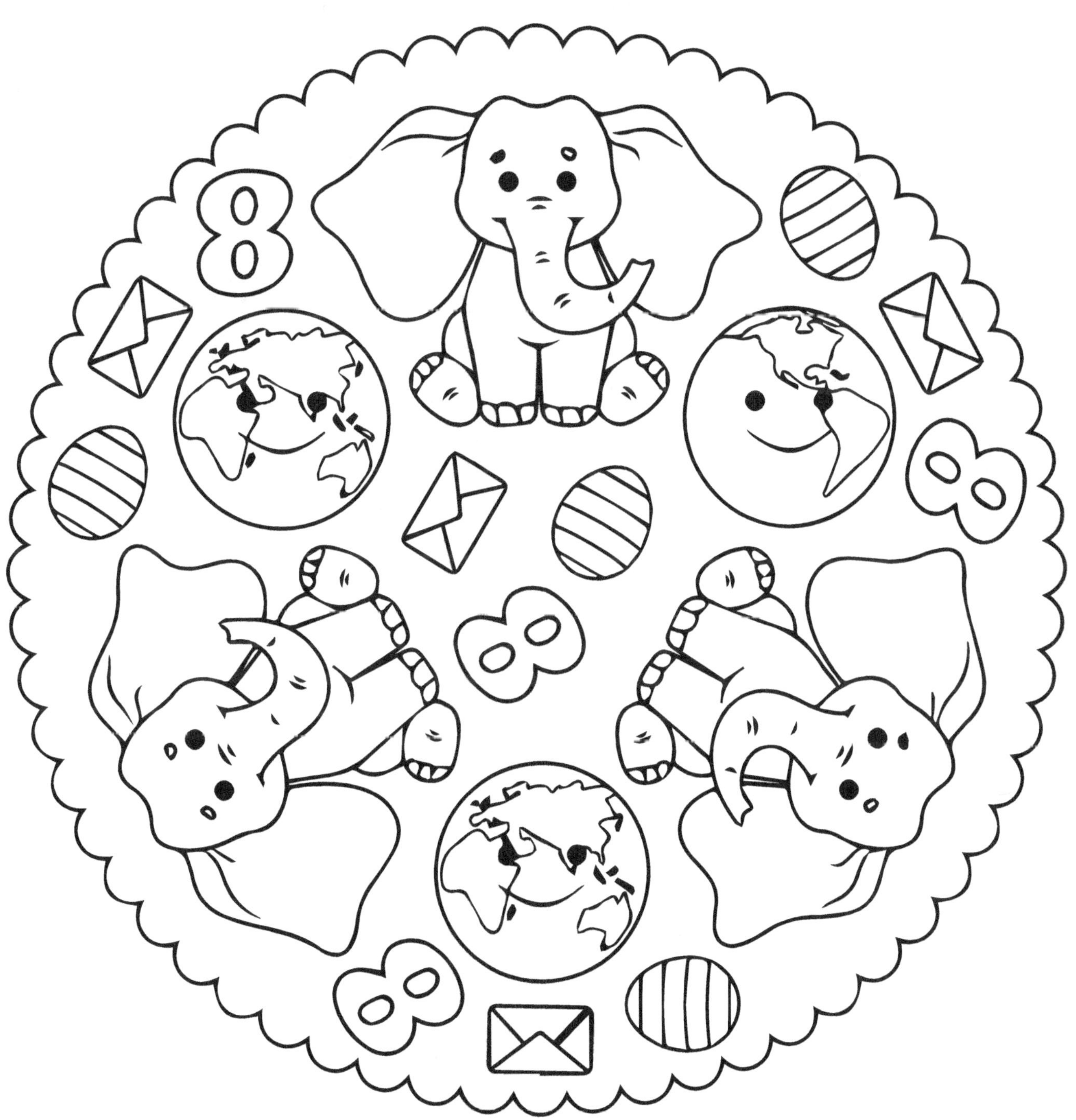

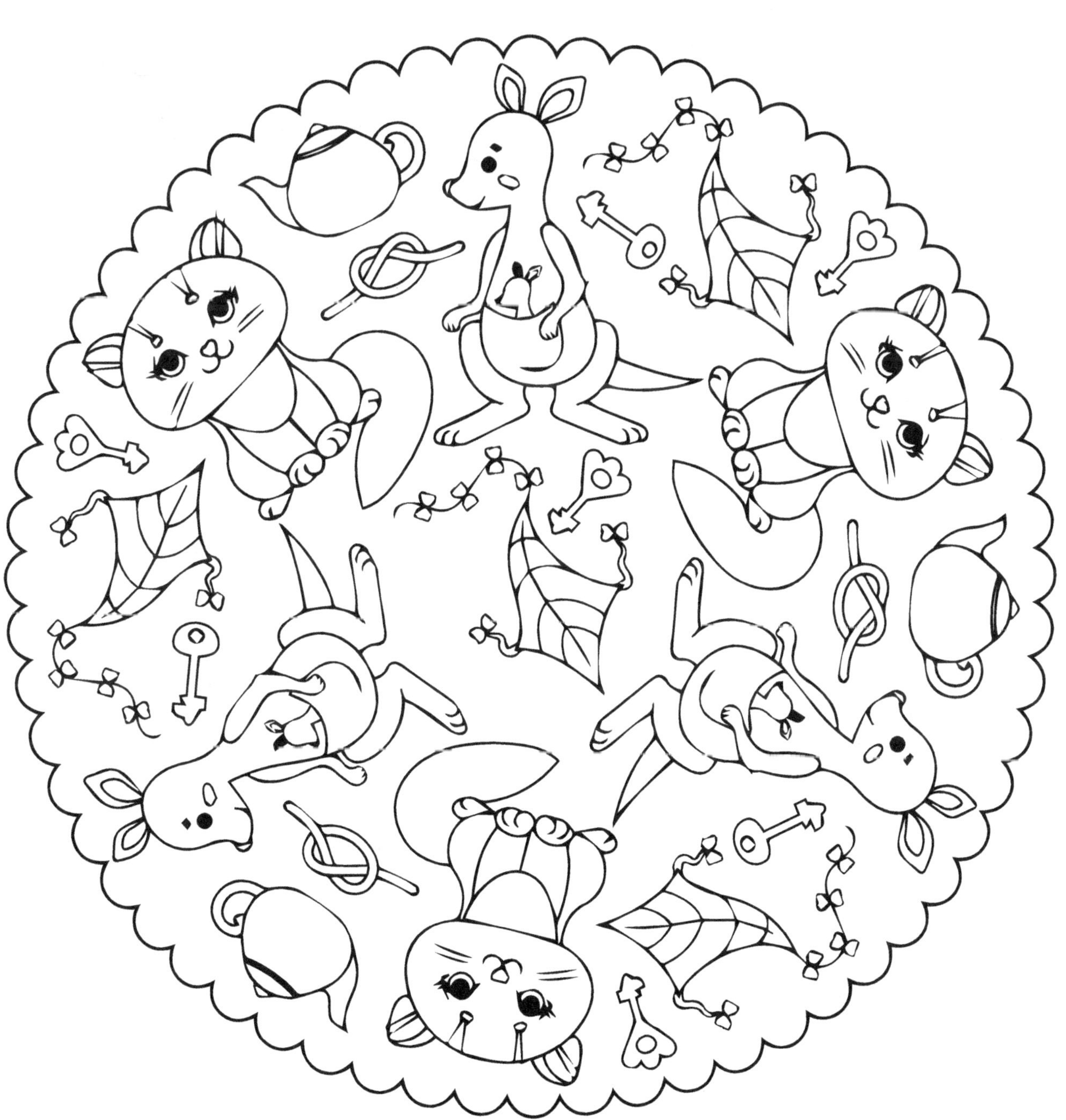

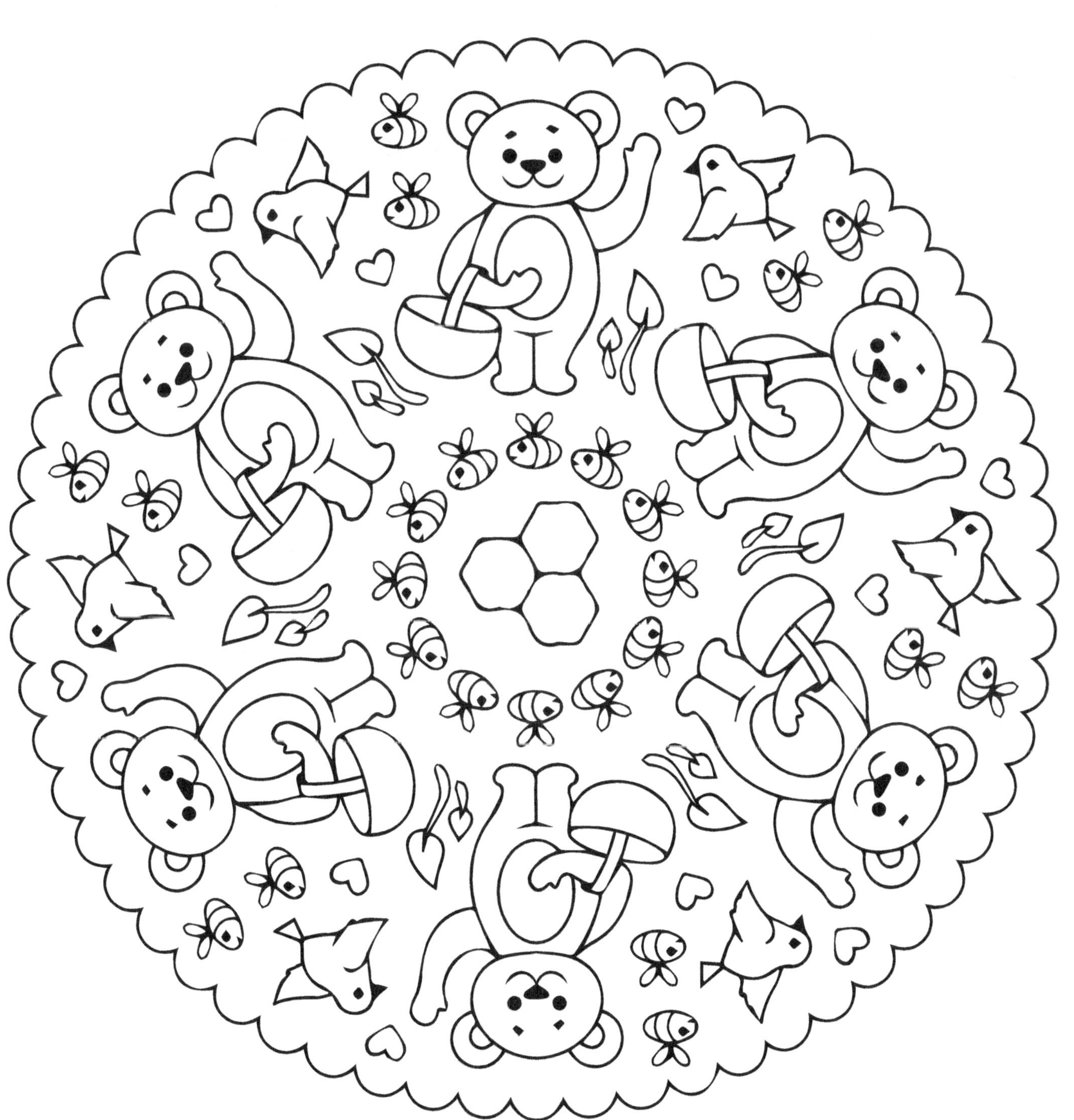

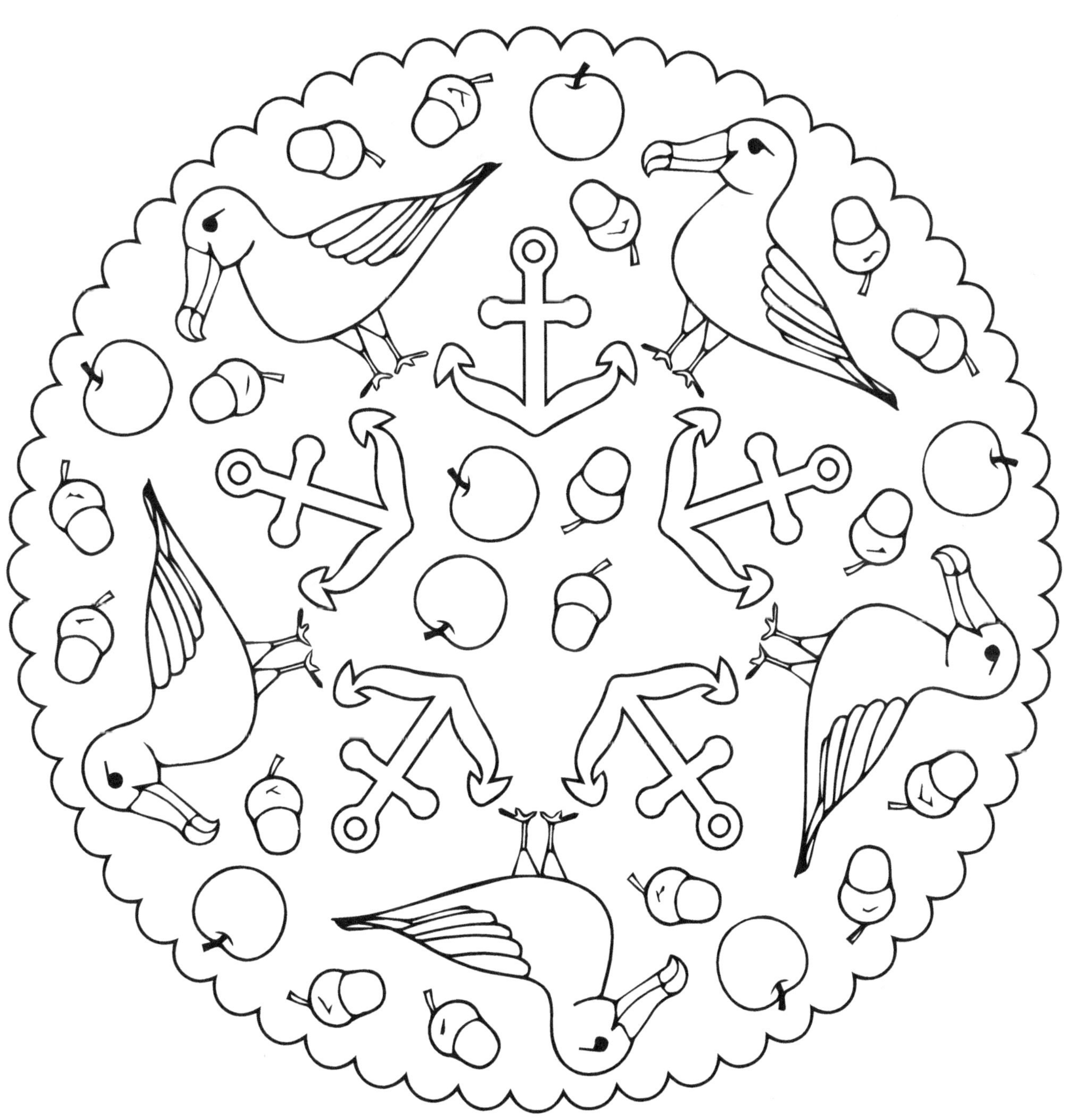

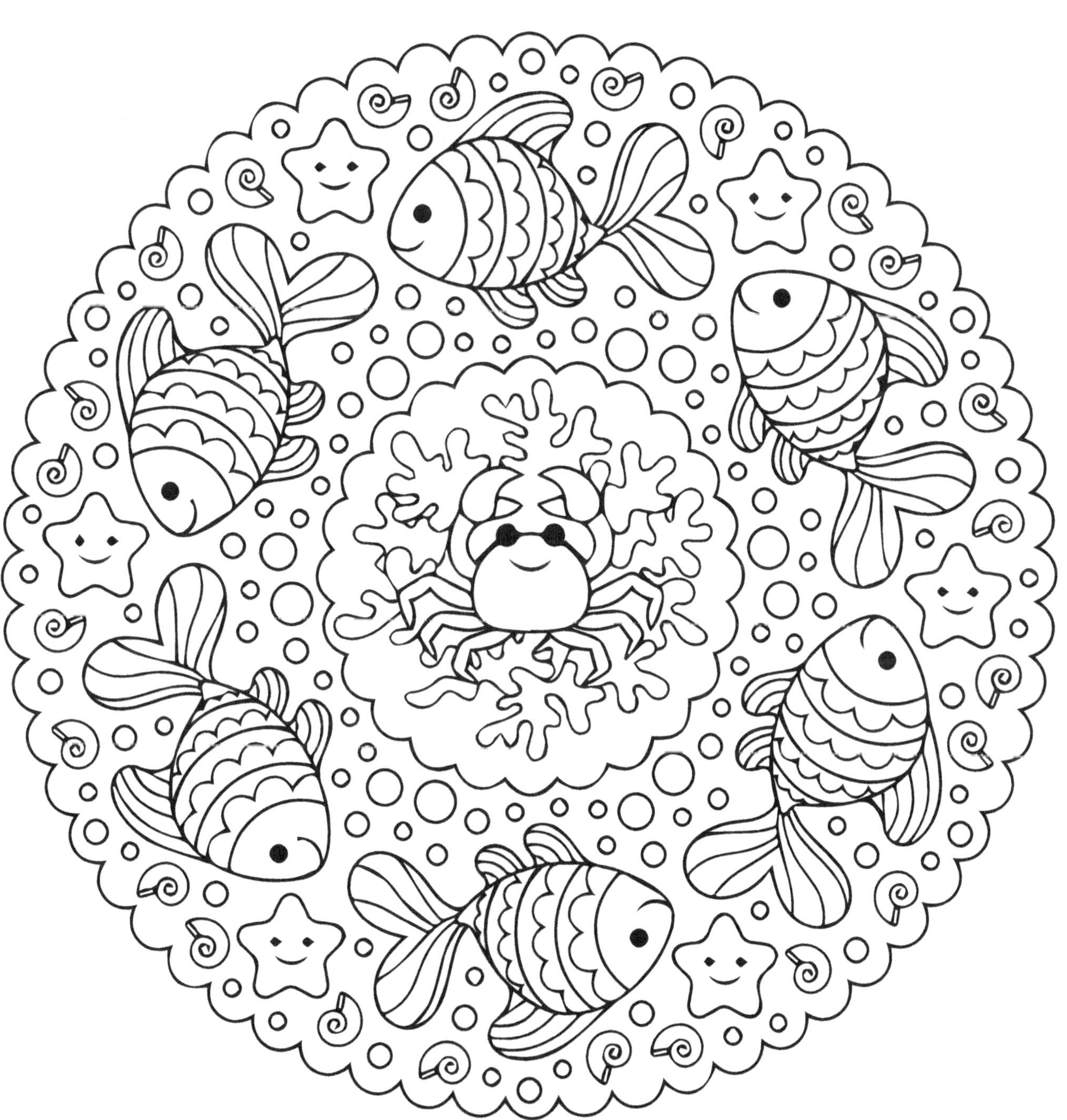

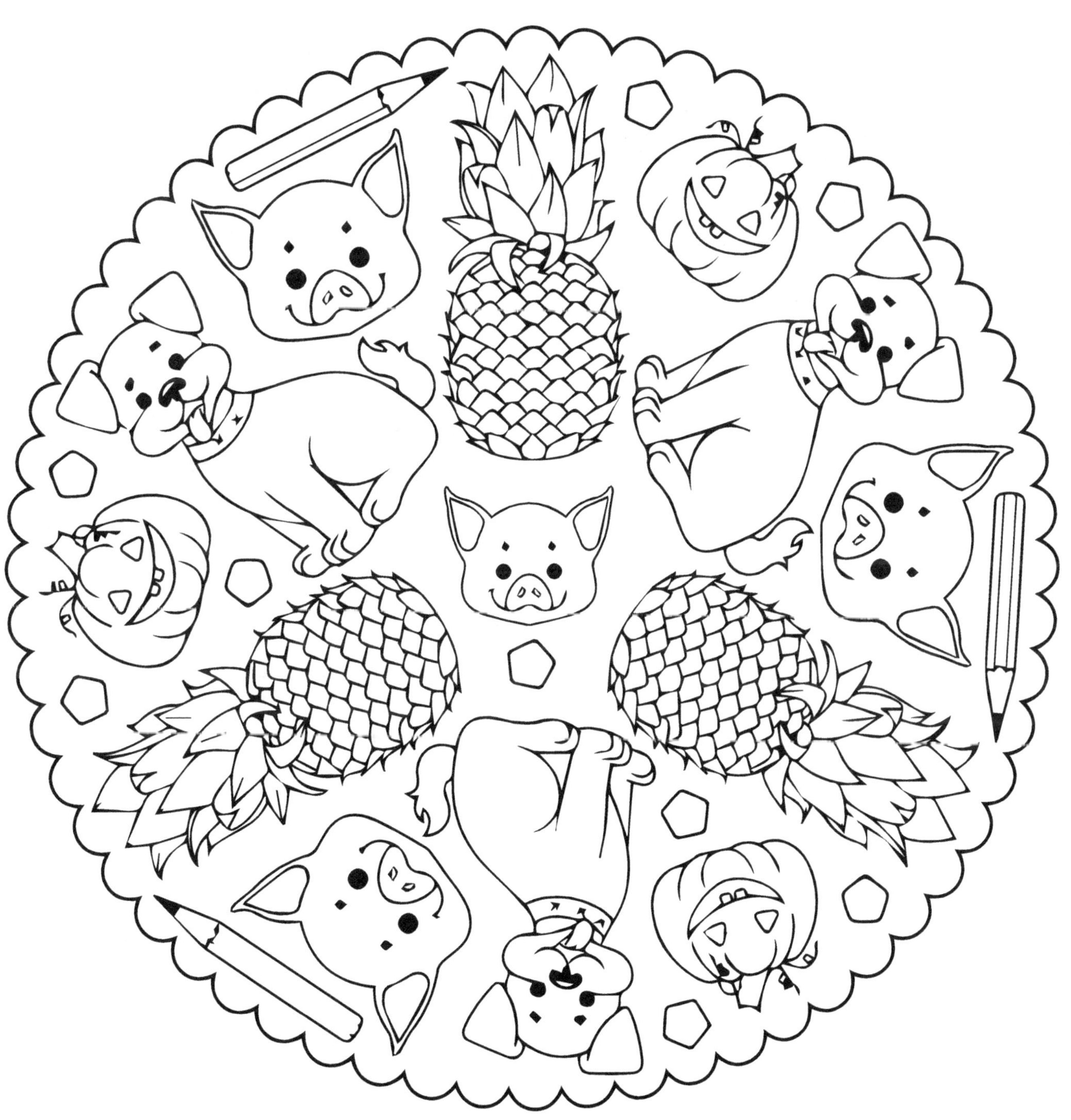

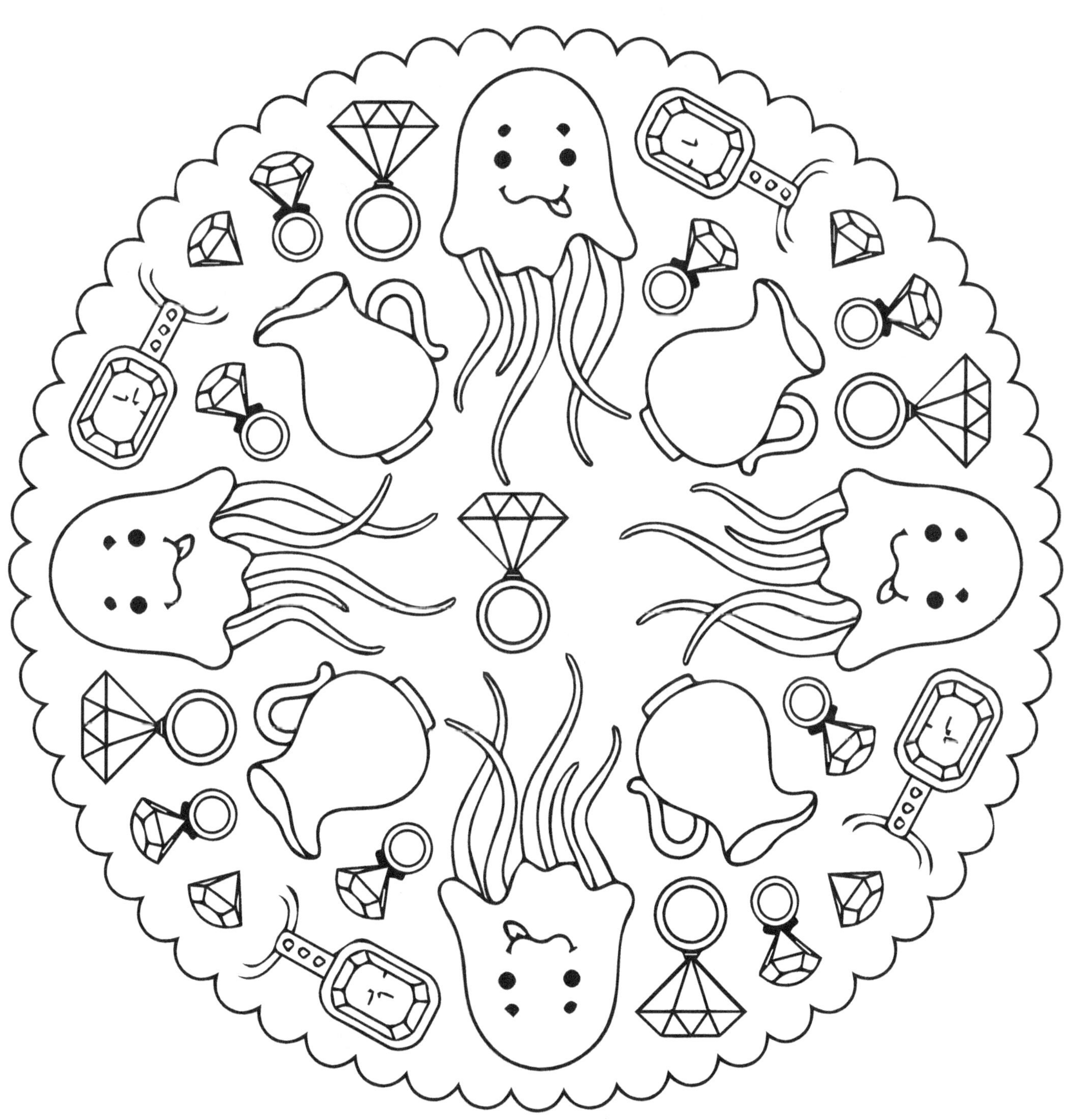

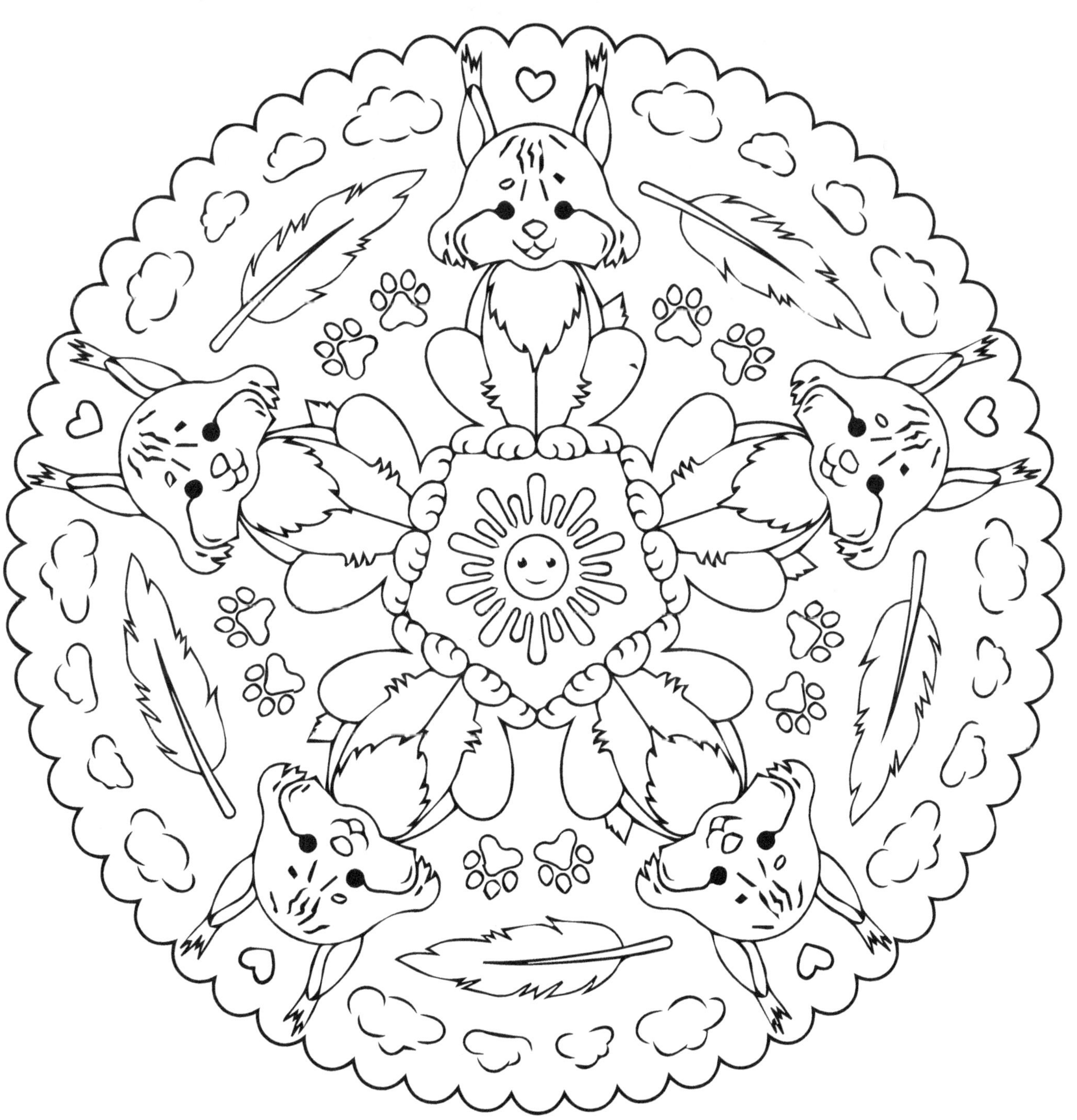

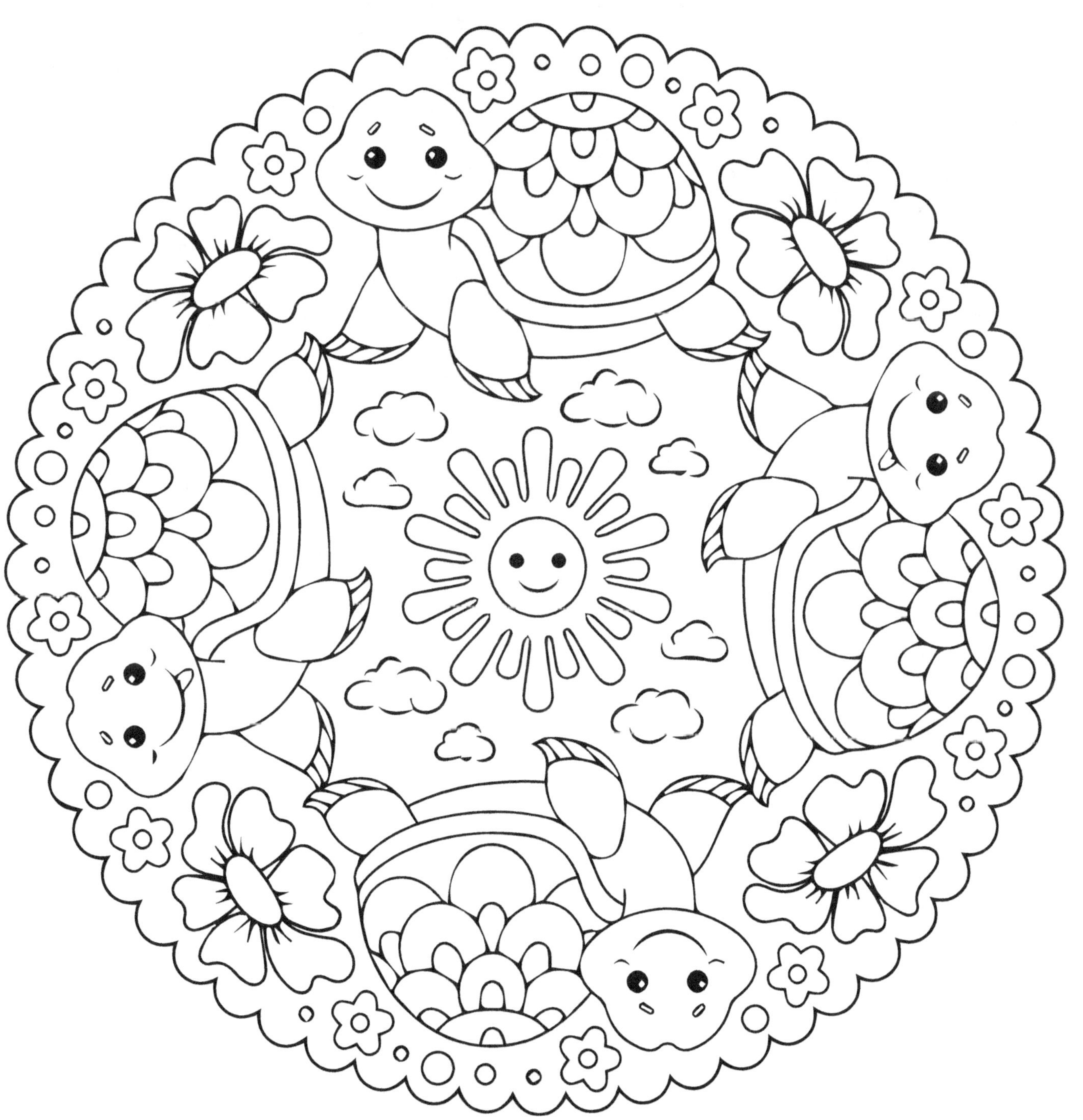

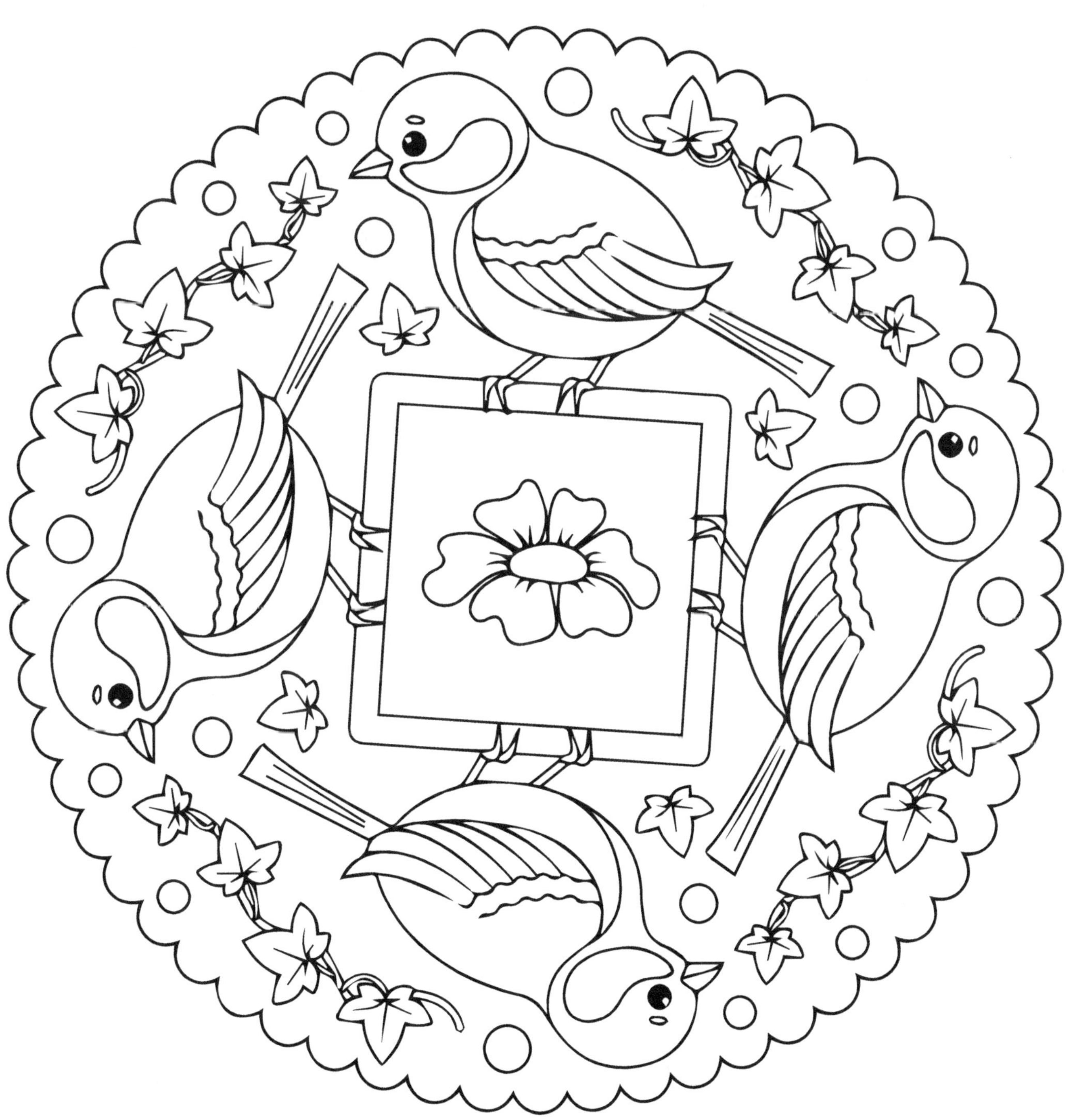

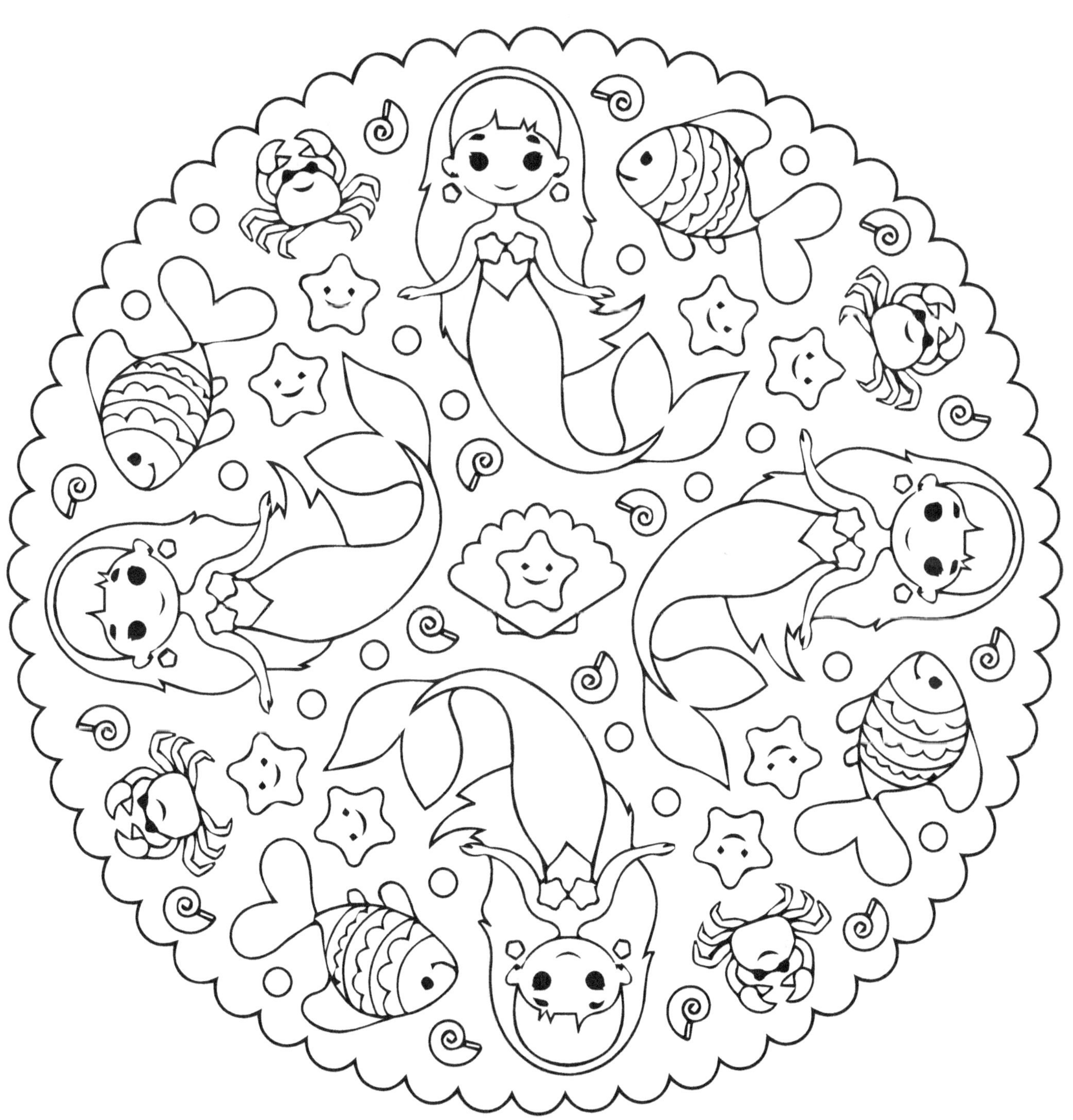

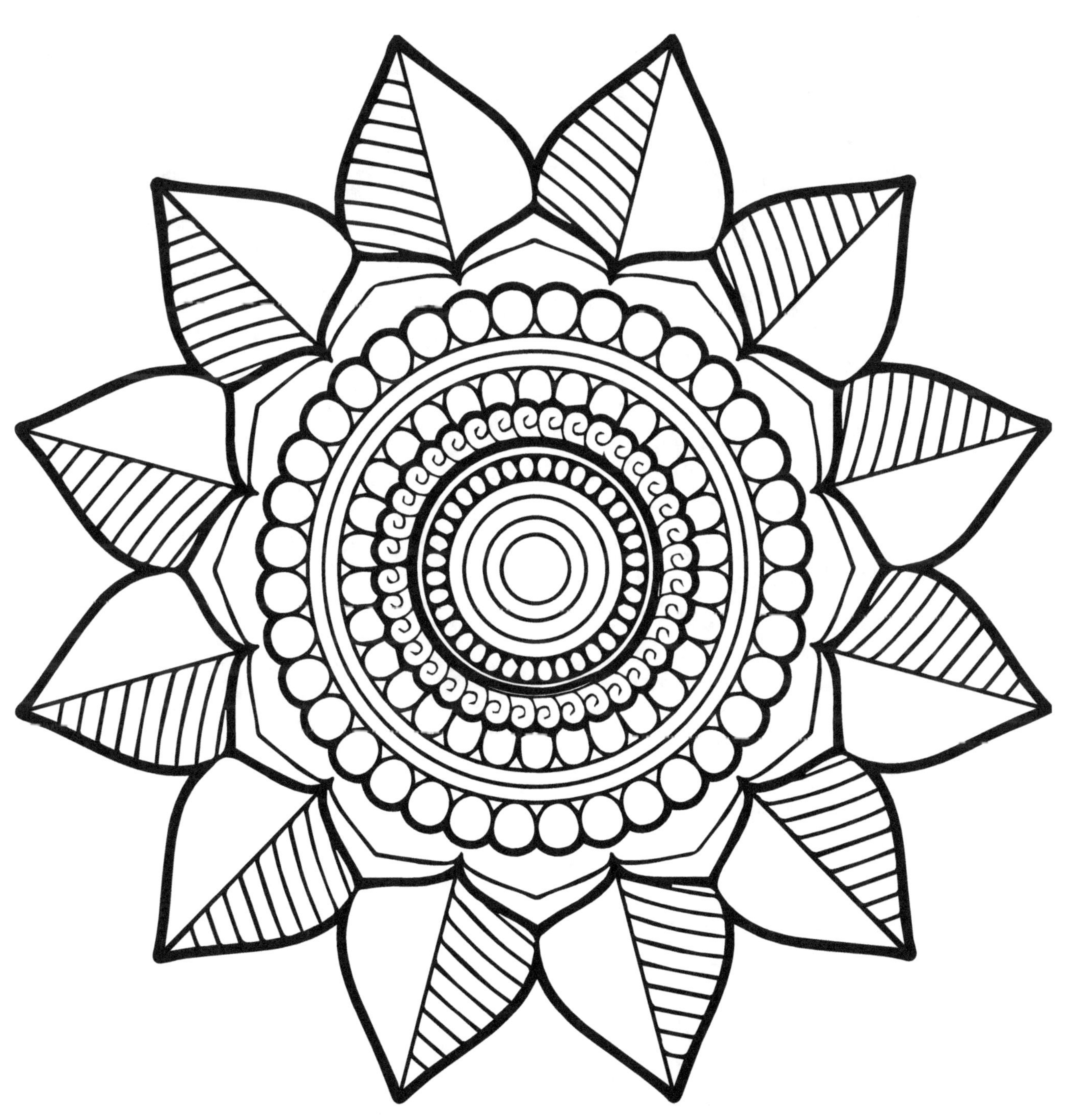

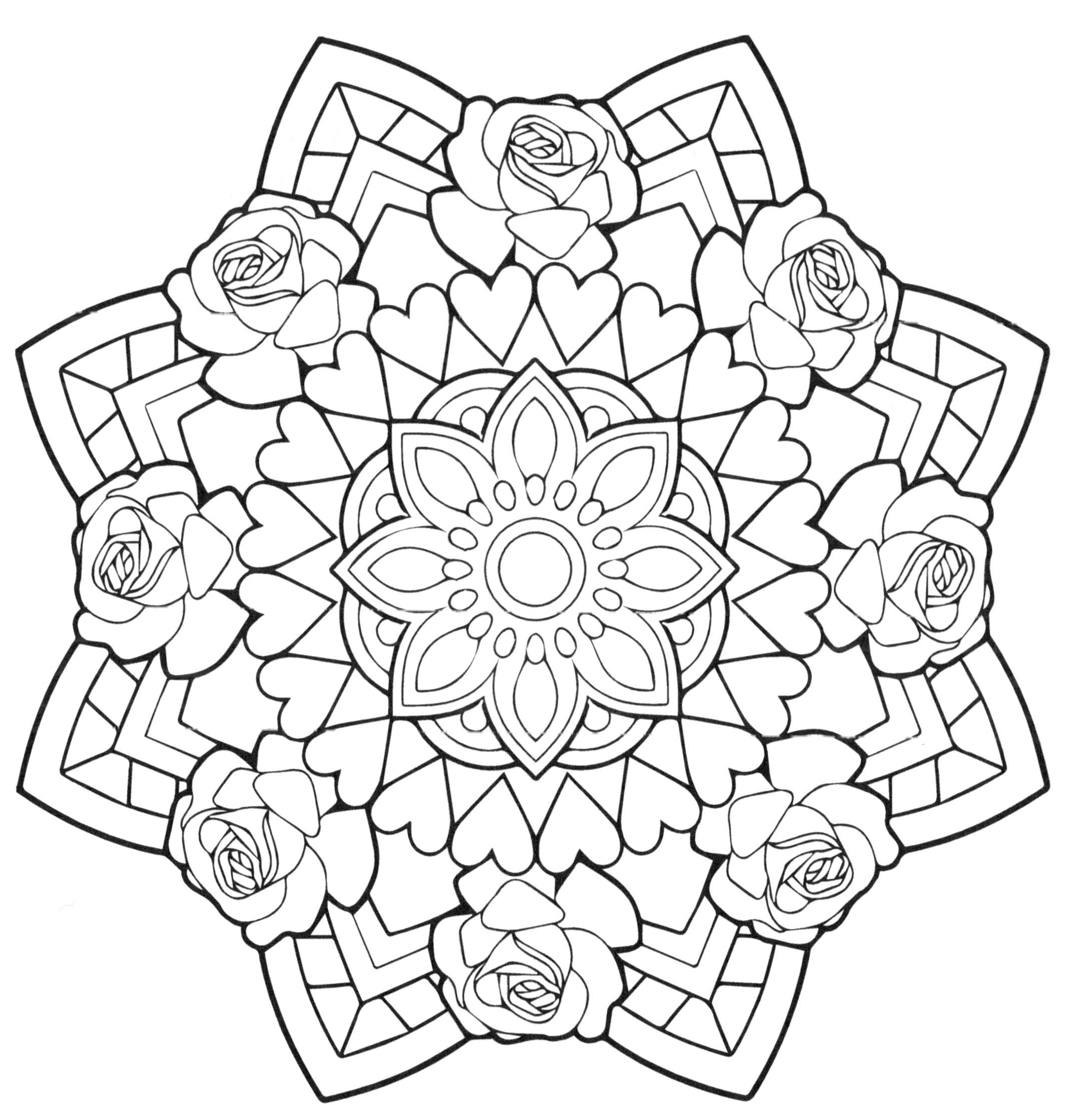

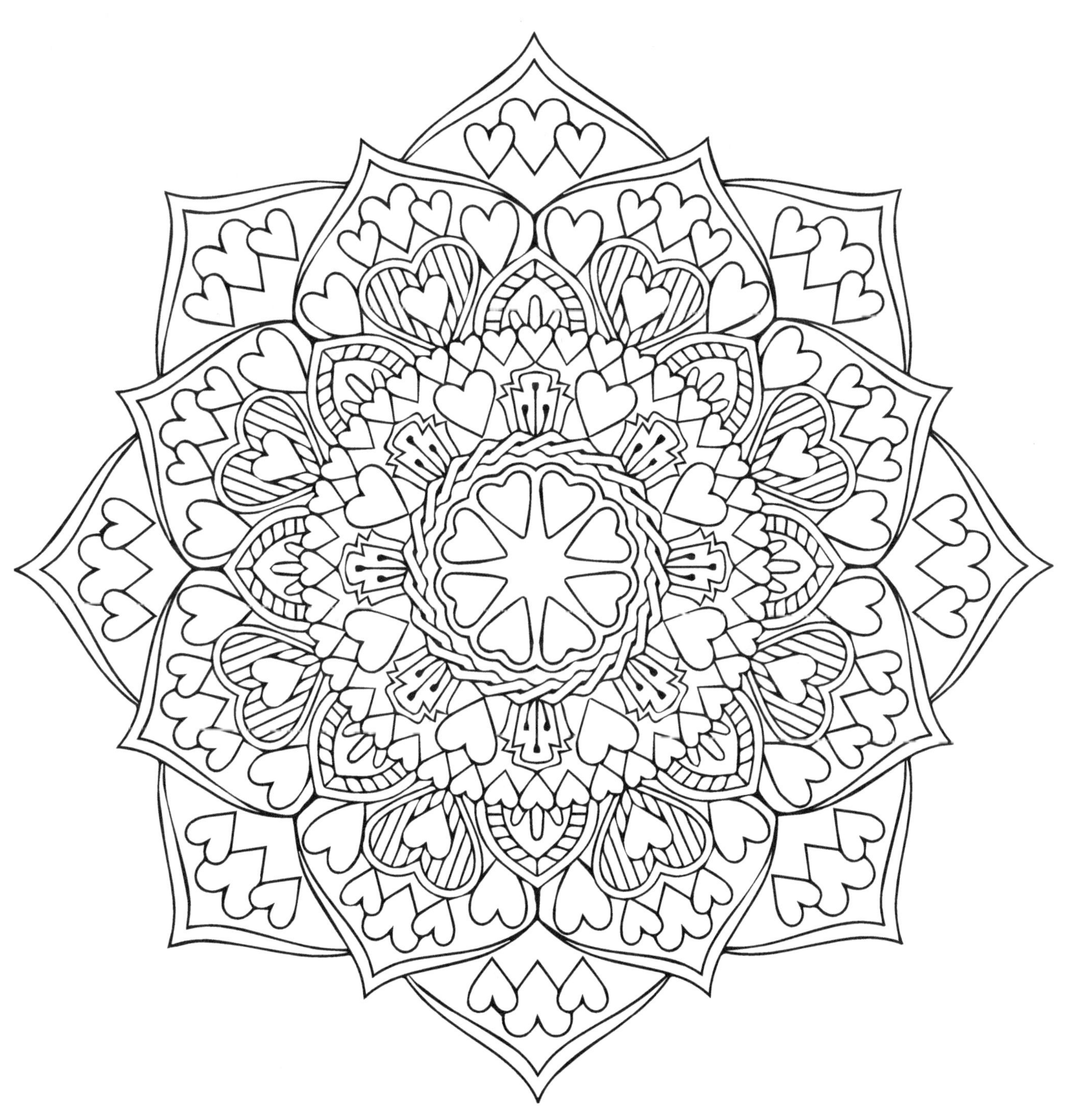

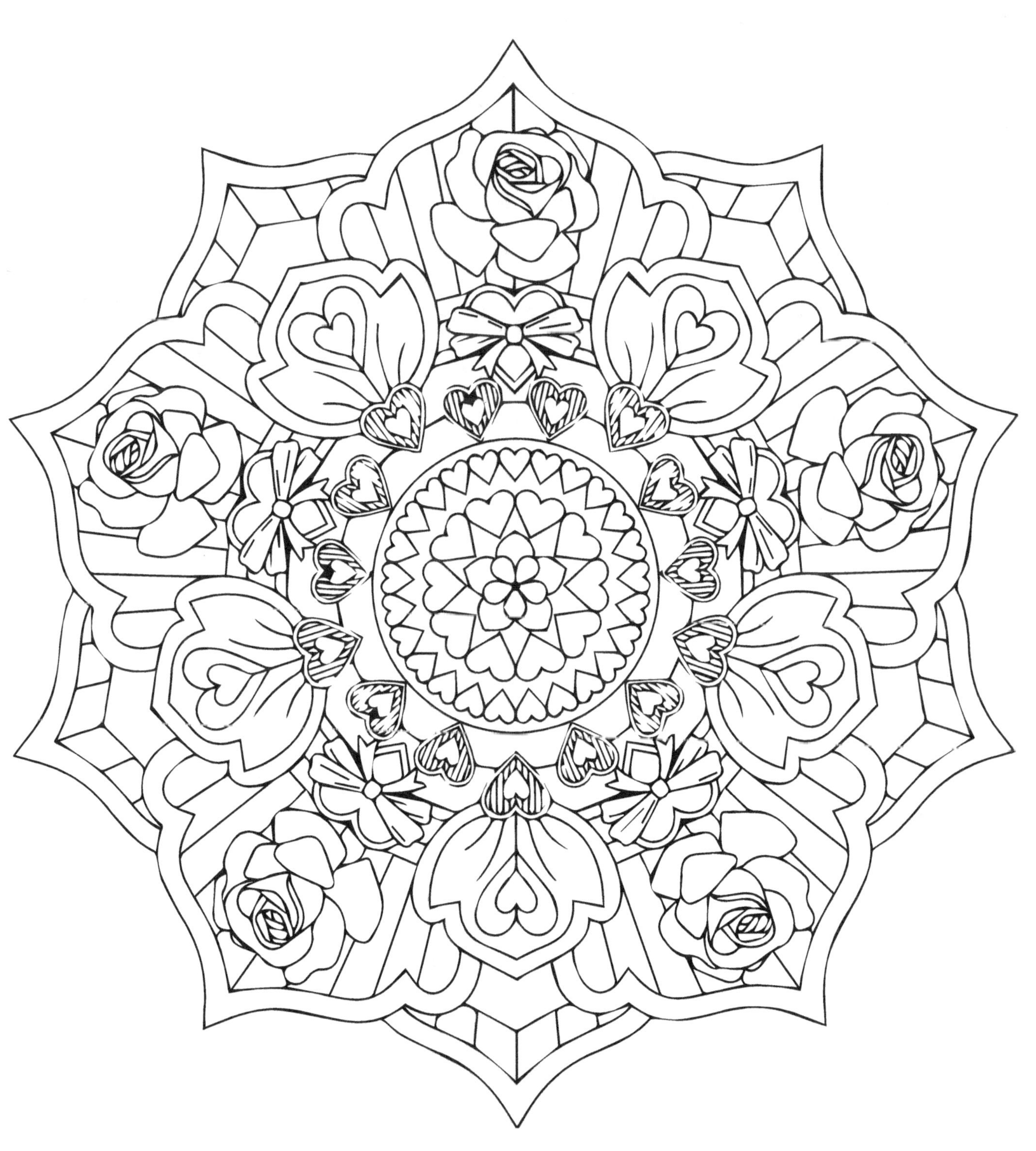

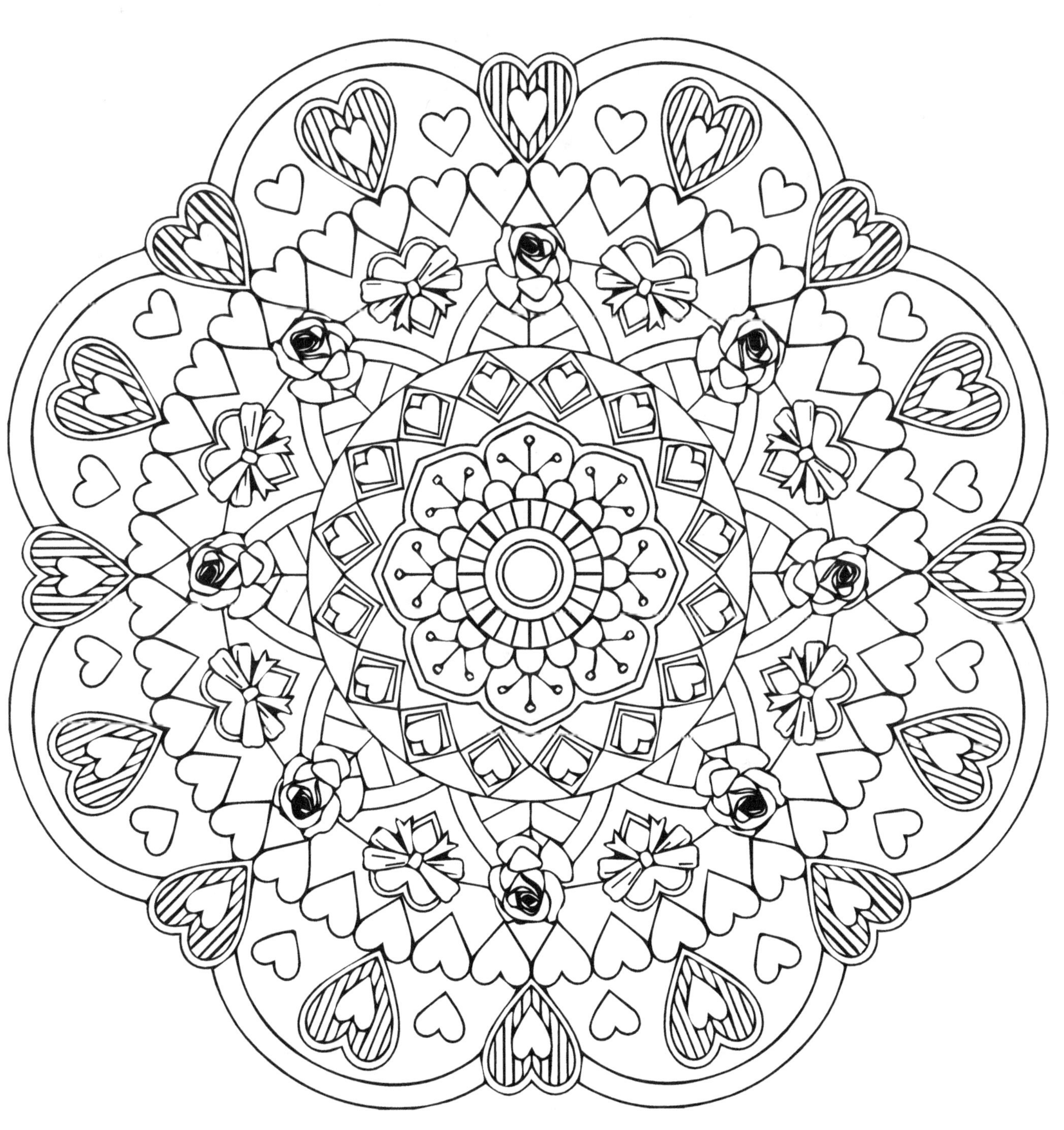

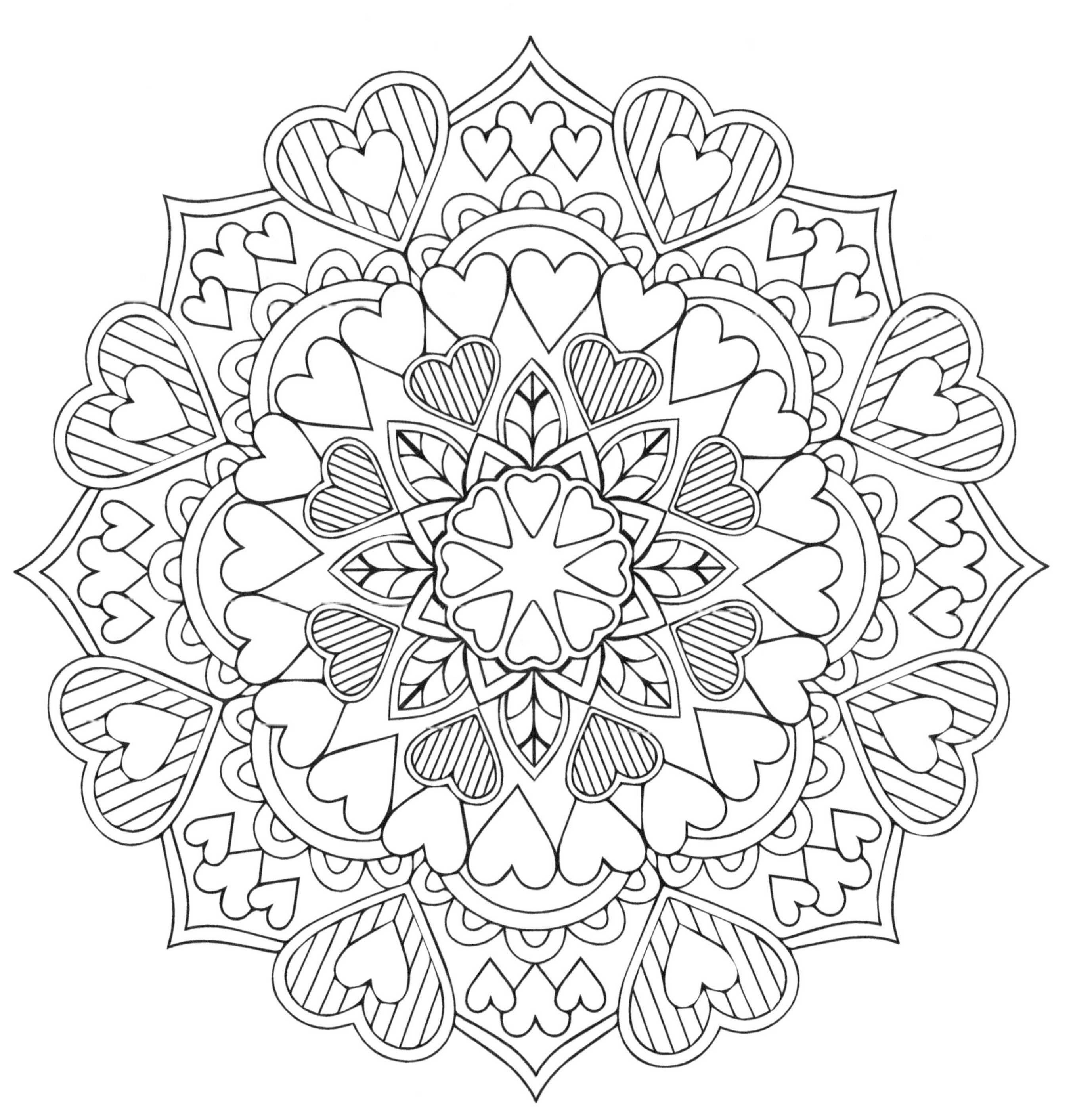

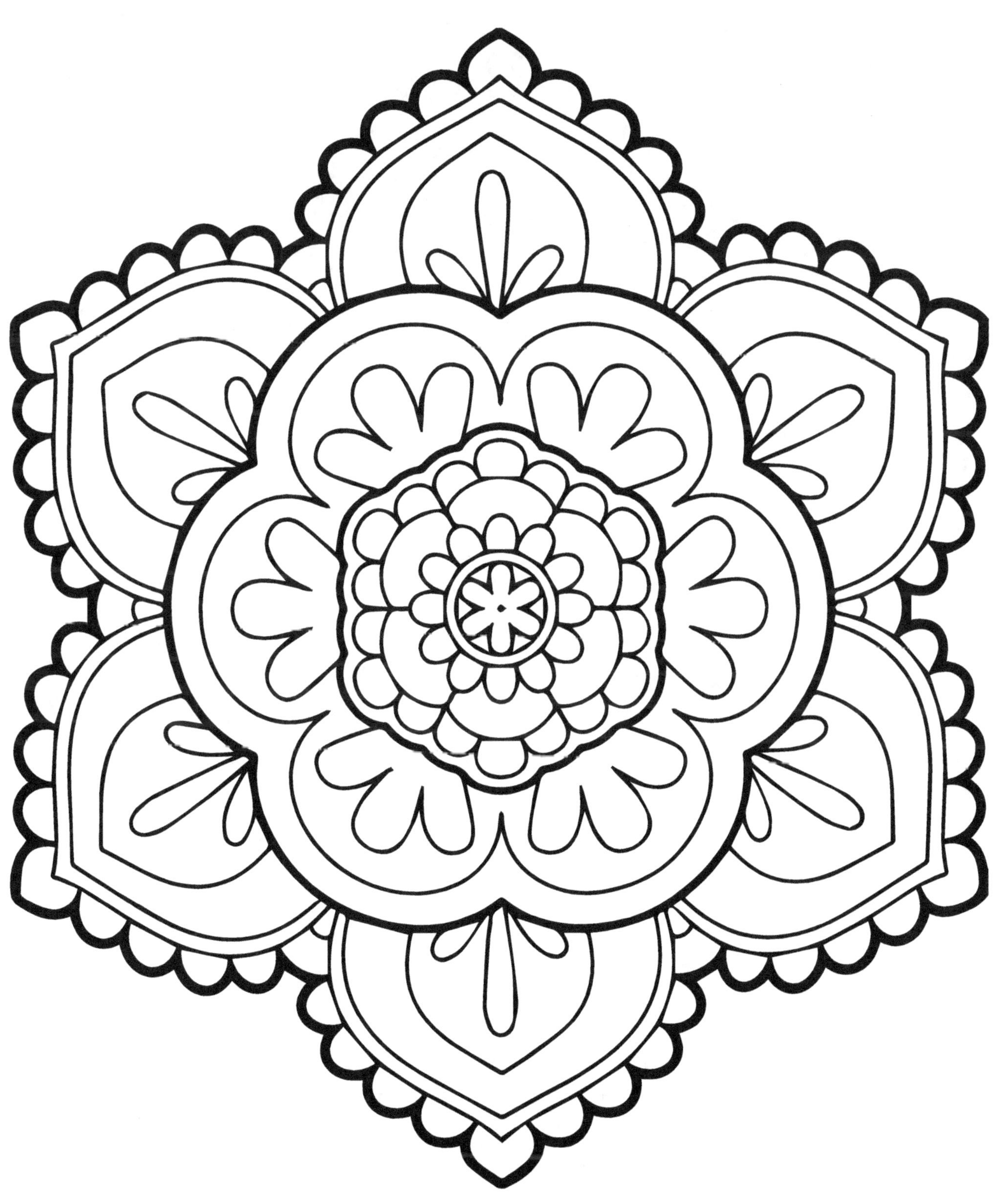

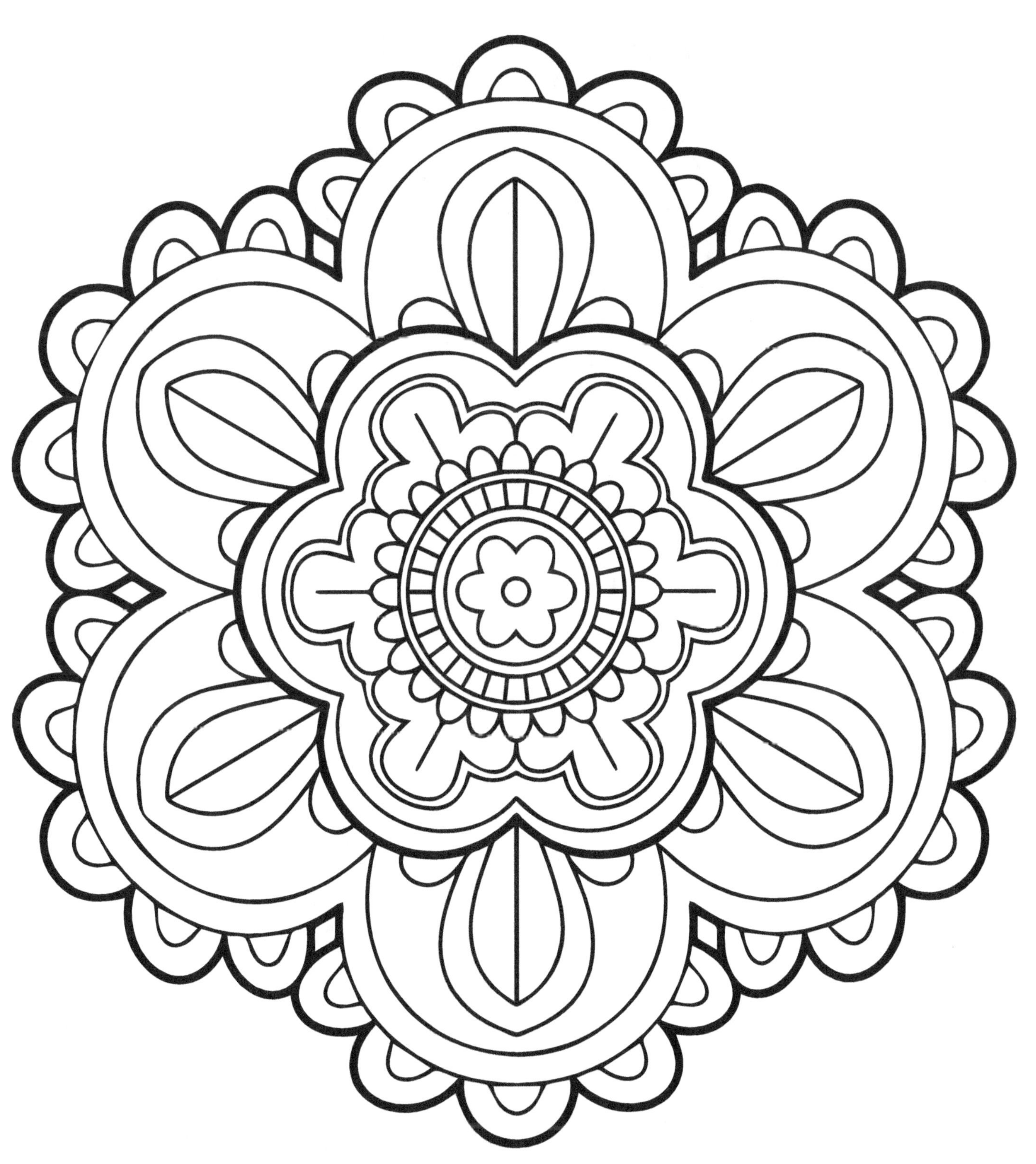

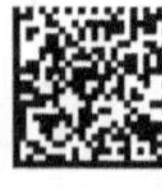

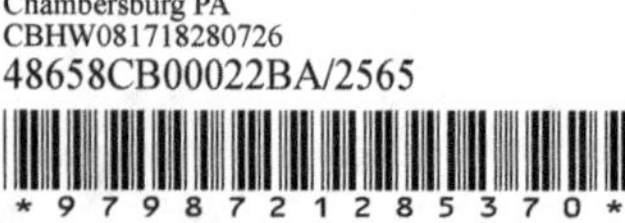
9 798721 285370